Our spirits soar as
On The Wings
Of Eagles

Fellowship Square-Tucson

D1511156

Printed in the United States of America.
U.S. Press & Graphics
Tucson, Arizona
(520) 886-7737 • www.uspress1.com

Our spirits soar as

On The Wings Of Eagles

Fellowship Square-Tucson

Compiled and edited by members of
the Golden Quill Pens Club
Writer's Group

Introduction

"Our spirits are raised as on the wings of eagles and made to shine like the sun!"

Paraphrased from Psalm 91, this powerfully uplifting thought eloquently expresses the opportunities that we have here at Fellowship Square Tucson

We have divided this book into chapters, with each chapter being independent of the others. Each chapter describes the spirit of ours from a slightly different perspective. The chapters collectively show that our lives here represent not the end, but the beginning…an opportunity to fulfill our potential, to be a viable part of our society.

Fellowship Square Tucson is a part of Christian Care Companies, a not for profit organization that is dedicated to providing *"…Quality, Affordable and Responsive Senior Housing…"* for their residents.

A Special Thanks

To the many talented people who have so generously given of their time and talent to help make this "dream" a reality. A special thanks goes to Alvin Brewer, George Gardiner, Toni Smith, and Charles Stone, along with all the men and women who are members of our Golden Quill Pens writers group; through whose tireless efforts have brought together the wonderful stories, poems and pictures included within. Through their abilities, many have been given the opportunity to have a voice and share their stories and creativity with others, and allow us all to *"Soar on the wings of Eagles…"*

Table of Contents

Introduction v

A Special Thanks v

CHAPTER ONE: "Our Spirits Soar" 2

    A HOUSE IS NOT A HOME 3

    ARIZONA HOME 4

    A TYPICAL DAY AT FELLOWSHIP SQUARE 5

    AMERICA 6

    BLESSINGS 7

    BLIND TO LIFE 8

    CACTUS CHRISTMAS 9

    CELESTIAL MUSIC 10

    CHANUKAH 10

    CHRISTMAS EVE 11

    CHRISTMAS LIST 1982 12

    DESERT NIGHT 13

    DREAMING 13

    EMBLEM OF LIBERTY 14

    IN RETROSPECT 14

    END OF THE RAINBOW? AN ETHEREAL POEM 15

    FREEDOM FLAG 16

    GIVING 17

    GIVING THANKS AND WHY WE SHOULD 18

    INCIDENT AT THE TRAIN STATION 19

    I'D RATHER 20

    LET THERE BE LIGHT! 21

    LADY LIBERTY 23

    MEMORIAL DAY 23

    NOVEMBER DAYS 24

    OVERFLOW 24

RANDOM THOUGHTS 25

SAFE HARBORS 26

SEPTEMBER 11TH, 2001 27

SISTERS IN CHRIST 28

SUPPOSE 28

THANKFUL.. 29

THE BREAK OF DAY 30

THE MAGIC OF MUSIC 31

THE RIGHT WORDS AT THE RIGHT TIME 34

THE WILD BLUE YONDER 35

TO CLIMB A RAINBOW 36

TUCSONAN'S LOVE THE RAIN.. 37

WHERE IS CHRISTMAS?.. 38

'TWAS THE NIGHT 40

CHAPTER TWO: "Birds Of A Feather" **42**

A SECRETARY'S TRAVEL TALE... 43

AN INTERESTING LADY 45

AVA'S FULL TIME DEVOTION 47

BILL'S UNPLANNED SOJOURN 49

BLUE CEILING... 51

I HAVE HAD A BLAST… 53

LOVABLE "D'S" 55

MEMORIES OF MIRIAM LEVITAN SPECTOR...................... 57

MEET THE BREWERS' 59

WHAT WERE YOU? 60

SOMETHING VERY SPECIAL SMOOTH—NICE AND HOT!
FRESHLY BREWED AND POURED DIRECTLY FROM THE
POT (THAT POURS TWO CUPS AT ONCE!)........................... 61

THE WALKERS AND TALKERS 62

STRONG TIES 63

THE APPEAL OF APPLAUSE 65

Table of Contents

THE GOOD LIFE.. 67

THE PIPER OF FELLOWSHIP SQUARE............................. 69

CHAPTER THREE: "On Leaving The Nest" **72**

ANTHONY... 73

BERMUDA 74

BOUNCING BETTY'S... 75

CHIVALRY IS DEAD 76

HOUSE FOR SALE 77

GETAWAYS 78

IF I COULD SING 78

LEARNING ABOUT ANTIQUES 79

LITTLE SOLDIER 81

LOVE HAPPENS 82

MOOCHIE SQUIRREL AND THE THANKSGIVING NUT 83

STILL...TWO 84

THE DAY WE BECAME AMERICANS 85

THOSE WERE THE DAYS 86

THE HOUSE 87

THE NEW WEST 89

TIME HAS NOT BEEN KIND 91

YEARLY AND DEARLY 92

CHAPTER FOUR: "A Flight Of Fancy" **94**

A DREAM TO DREAM... 95

AN ORGAN RECITAL.. 96

ANOTHER CHRISTMAS 97

CHAIR DANCING 98

GOD (HE MAY HAVE FEELINGS, TOO!)............................ 99

HAIKU.. 100

JEFFERSON 101

Table of Contents

I NEED TIME!!! 103

MAMA KITTY 104

MY FIRST DATE IN FIFTY YEARS! 105

MVD 106

NEWCOMER 106

OBSERVATIONS 107

OUT MY WINDOW 108

OF MICE AND MEN 109

REMEMBERING 111

PARKING SPACE... 113

SHOULDA STOOD IN BED 114

THAT'S A LOT OF BULL.. 115

SIMPLE PLEASURES 116

THE FEAT OF DRESSING MY FEET 117

THE GAME... 118

THE UNCERTAIN QUARK 119

TRIVIAL PURSUIT 120

VIEWPOINT 121

WORDS 122

WE ARE OUR SERENE HIGHNESS PAULINA 123

WHEN IN ROME DO AS THE ROMANS DO 125

WHITE STUFF 126

CHAPTER FIVE: "How High The Sky" **128**

A CLOCK'S NOT TIME! 129

ARE WE WINNING THE RACE? 130

BETTER LUCK NEXT YEAR.. 131

ENVIRO CRISIS——DO WE CARE?................................. 132

EXISTENTIALISM 133

EXPECTATIONS 134

Table of Contents

FREE WILL...135

GOD'S PALETTE 136

IN PRAISE OF THE SOUTHWEST 137

JOURNEY FROM SHOWER TO THE EASY CHAIR 138

JUST A FEW WORDS ABOUT TUCSON DRIVERS 139

LOLA AND PAT..141

PRAYER AT EVENING 142

REFLECTED GLORY 142

THE COMPANY YOU KEEP 142

THE COLORS OF ARIZONA................................143

THE CATALINAS..144

THE MISSING TURTLE 145

TO DREAM..146

TORTOISE WINS RACE WHILE THE HARE IS SLEEPING 147

UNDAUNTED 149

VOODOO WOMAN 150

CHAPTER SIX: "Shine Like The Sun" **152**

A LETTER TO LENORE....................................153

A NEW BROOM 154

A VISIT IN THE DARK 155

DIANA..156

BOB HOPE'S BROTHER 157

HARRY TRUMAN 159

HIDDEN FEELINGS 161

IS THERE AN EXCUSE? 162

LIFE AT THE END OF A RAINBOW 165

LOVE IN COLOR..166

MAKING A DIFFERENCE: OR ONE STEP AT A TIME!.......167

MY FIRST ICE CREAM CONE..............................168

Table of Contents

MY LOVE SONG FOR EVERY DAY 168

MY VALENTINE... 169

ODE TO A DEAD POET 170

ROMEO AND JULIET 171

THANKFULNESS 171

THE TOP OF THE HILL 172

TO TUCSON 173

TURTLE ON A FENCE POST: OR THE UNSEEN HAND 174

CHAPTER SEVEN: "Our Spirits Challenged" 176

AN EXTRAORDINARY PLACE 177

A SECOND CHANCE 179

AND THE BAND PLAYED ON! 180

CHRISTMAS CHEER 181

GREEN WAS IN 182

REMINISCING 183

"SOMETHING" IN THE AIR 185

THE BUSY LEPRECHAUNS 186

UNDER A CASINO SKY 187

WHAT'S BREWING 189

WINDS OF CHANGE 190

CHAPTER EIGHT: "Reflections From On High" 198

24 FUZZBALLS ALL IN A ROW 199

AFTER THE RAIN 202

A VISIT TO THE LAZY RR 203

ALONE BUT NOT LONELY 205

AS TIME GOES BY 206

DOWN SIZING 207

HOUSEWIVES AND POETRY 208

LAMENT 208

Table of Contents

LIFE IN TEXAS – THE EARLY YEARS 209

LIGHTS OUT 211

LOVER RECONSIDERED 214

MORNING 215

MUSIC...216

OLD FOLKS 217

PEANUT BUTTER 219

REFLECTIONS..220

SHEPHERD HOUSE—ADAM 221

SWEET YESTERDAY 222

THE HIGH COST OF LIVING 223

THE NEW NEIGHBOR 224

THE HOTTEST SPOT 224

THE OLD HOME PLACE...225

TRIBUTE TO OUR MAILMAN 227

TREE CORNER 229

WINTER JEWELS 230

CHAPTER NINE: "Down To Earth" 232

CLANCY 233

CONSIDERING 235

LADY-IN-WAITING...236

EXCERPTS FROM MEMORIES & IMAGINATION 237

MERRY BIRTHDAY 240

MERRY OCTOBER FIRST 241

NEWCOMER 242

OTHER COUSINS AND OTHER BROTHERS 243

RE-CYCLE 244

THE DRUID FACTOR 245

THE FIRST TIME I SAW QUEEN ELIZABETH 247

Table of Contents

THE PROPHETIC INDIAN CHIEF 248

THE MAGIC WAND 249

THE SKY MAY BE FALLING 251

THE TEMPERANCE SERMON 253

TRAVEL ON THE AIRLINE 254

WARNING 255

CHAPTER TEN: "In The Spirit Of Appreciation" **258**

WITH APPRECIATION 259

THE LEGACY OF THE CROOKED TREE
OF FELLOWSHIP SQUARE 260

TO CHARLES STONE, WITH GRATITUDE 261

THANKS FOR THE OPPORTUNITY 262

CONTRIBUTORS 263

CHAPTER ONE

Our Spirits Soar

When our spirits are up-lifted, we get a new perspective…an enthusiastic appreciation of life.

The following stories and poems reflect the inspirational moments that contribute so much to that full and meaningful life.

A HOUSE IS NOT A HOME
By Oreita Smith

The time was 1954, and my new husband convinced me, shortly after our marriage, that he wanted to live on a ranch and that I would agree if I saw it. He had already bought a ten acre ranch in Washington State, about 25 miles out of the city. I had not set eyes on the place but tried to be optimistic. On the way to this idealistic place he described the property to me – "a red barn, a trout farm next door, a creek running across the back five acres, and a chicken house 24x60".

I knew I had not heard a house described, so I was not surprise when we arrived to in fact see no house!!

He suggested we might want to clean out the chicken house (as opposed to the larger barn) and live there until we could build a house. In the face of no electricity, bath facilities, running water or insulation, no cabinets nor closets I began to be discouraged. Especially thinking about the cold Washington winters! Our only heat was a blue and chrome wood burning stove. It fell my duty to care for the livestock: heifers, chickens, ducks, sheep, geese, and pigs. This did nothing for my morale and after two years, frustrated to the point of suicide I left.

Fast forward to 1959 – I had met and married a wonderful man, a career Army Sergeant. And spend the next 35 year with him happily. Our first post was Ft. Huachuca, and after his one tour in Korea we went to Missouri, then to Germany, then to Ft. Lewis, Washington. My three children and I stayed behind while he served in Vietnam. Then to Ft. Sheridan, Ill. Our last tour was where we started, Ft. Huachuca.

I enjoyed being a career Army wife and also enjoyed our trips around the country in our travel trailer after his retirement. Ten years ago he became ill with cancer and died about a year after becoming ill.

I am enjoying my new home at Fellowship Square and my many friends here and those I have known for some time as well.

ARIZONA HOME
By Frances McCreadie

Like a sentinel on a silent hill
Of Indian bands that roam
The tall Saguaro gazes still
Upon my desert home.
The wild terrain is just the same
As ages long ago
Under a blazing turquoise sky;

           May it be ever so!

My entrance door swings doubly wide.
As friendly doors should do,
To bring a double welcome to
My friends who enter through;
A beckoning arm, the hallway
Leads to the left—to right
A gently snoring Doberman

           Lies in the firelight.

At twilight, through the window wall
Or from the patio,
The rugged Catalinas
Mirror sunset's glow;
The evening star will hover
As the western sky grows dim.
O! May God's blessing cover

           All those who dwell within.

A TYPICAL DAY AT FELLOWSHIP SQUARE—By Charlie Stone

In the morning I awake to a most pleasant sound.
Someone's cutting my grass, you see!
Just why that it pleases my ears, I've found;
Is simply that the someone's not me!

I open the door, and low and behold,
See an incredible, wonderful color array
Of every conceivable flower unfold
In a dazzling, beautiful, efflorescent display.

Exercise classes start in the morning.
A sight you must see to believe it!
Arms and legs flailing every which way.
Find the pain and a way to relieve it.

As my joints limber up with a snap, crackle, pop,
My muscles think they're mistreated.
But, how good it feels when I eventually stop,
With my energy all but depleted!

We moan and we groan to be all we can be.
Our efforts are hardly half-hearted.
And after it's over, one thing we agree,
We're better off now than when we started!

The hot tub is next, or the pool is fun.
Either one you'll find most salubrious.
A generous mixture of water and sun….
If there's a better life anywhere, it's dubious!

Thoughts of their dinner cause my glands to react
In a manner that would make Pavlov smile.
You can count on their food, as a matter of fact,
To be a gourmet's delight served with style.

With an evening of bridge or a walk with a friend,
A movie or I go my own way,
I bring to a close, and a memorable end,
To what's turned out to be a great day!

When first I arrived, it seemed such a loss.
But, I realize now that I'm winning
A life filled with order instead of chaos,
And it's not really the end, but the beginning!

AMERICA
By Frances McCreadie

Out of his lofty eyrie,
Over the wild terrain,
The eagle's eye encompasses
His far and vast domain.

This symbol of our nation
Reminds us to be firm.
To guard what most we cherish
From those who would seek us harm.

So let us stand united,
And pledge our loyalty
That America, like the eagle,
Forever shall be free.

BLESSINGS
By Marion Brown

Joyeux Noel!

Shalom to all!

The spirit of love and peace

Does call,

And casts her glow

On all mankind;

Calling forth

Our soul's true nature.

Revealed in Scripture

Many centuries past,

Forever alive,

Within our hearts.

In any language

Its truth shines forth

And all hearts thrill

To its timeless message—

PEACE ON EARTH

BLESSINGS TO ALL

BLIND TO LIFE
By Alvin Brewer

Revenge is sweet, so the saying goes.
Yes, indulging the temptation to get even
Creates an eye for an eye and tooth for a tooth world.

After all, we are only balancing the scales.
You know, leaving no stone unturned in the
Act of leaving none unthrown.

In this exchange of retribution to which
So many make a contribution,
It's a wonder more people are not
Sightless and toothless.
We are so ruthless.
Yes, turning the cheek is just for the meek,
And giving your neighbors your cloak is a joke.

Oops, Our Beloved just sent me a note, and I quote:

"You've developed a bad habit.
These values don't belong to My Kingdom
On heaven or earth.
Where did you get them?
Please quit!

I own the scales, why do you do the judging?
Please stop begrudging My role.
My justice is based on My grace.
That's the only way you'll save face.
I recycle souls not their habits."

CACTUS CHRISTMAS
By Stella Klepac

It's a gentle Christmas
Here, among the palms and the cactuses
As gentle as those little cherubim clouds
That we see lazy-loafing over the mountains

It is not a time to bow our heads,
And hurry and scurry before the wind and snow;
Nor to cower in warm corners.

Nor do we need to slush along the icy streets,
Booted and bundled,
While making the happy preparations.

It is a time to wrap ourselves in sunshine,
And step boldly, with our heads high,
To indulge our sense with the sweet smells,
And the caroling of the birds.

To gaze into the lambent sky,
That heartbreaking blue—
To gaze idly upon the mountains,
Our mountains that ring us about,
Beyond them lies the world.

It's a sparkling Season
Here in the Southwest,
Where the garlands sparkle doubly
In the sun;
And haughty saguaros stand,
Disdaining the shining burden
That people have heaped upon them.

Where the night is a fairyland of colored lights;

Where the night is a glittering wonder,
With the diamond brightness of the stars—

It's a gentle Christmas
Here in Arizona…

CELESTIAL MUSIC
By Frances McCreadie

Crunching through the snow on a cold, starry night
Disheveled diamonds scatter at my feet.
While overhead unnumbered stars are shimmering their light
While marching to a universal beat.

In silence you may think that you can hear
The faintly rhythmic music of the spheres
In harmony while countless ages roll,
God sets the pathway under his control.

CHANUKAH—By Mimi Lloyd

The aroma of Potato Latkes (pancakes) crisping in the frying pan…the glow of the Menorah. Ah, yes, I remember it well, so the song says. This is because we as Jews, are celebrating a miracle that took place centuries ago. This holiday celebrates the victory of Judah the Maccabee against the Syrians. It was a religious victory of freedom. Freedom from imposing the worship of pagan idols, which the cruel Greek king Antiochus was trying to impose on all nationalities. The Jews refused to do this and fought against his rule and won a victory. In battle, the Temple was badly damaged, and needed to be rebuilt and re-dedicated. But there was a problem. They found that there was only one day's supply of oil left to light the holy lamp. (So…here's the miracle part.) the Menorah burned brightly for eight days.

This is why we light the Menorah for eight days. We say thanks and praise God for the miracle he wrought for our ancestors in ancient times. We eat food that reminds us of the oil used in the Temple. That is why the tradition of foods fried in oil is still observed. When the days have grown cold and night descends early, the darkest time of the year, the Festival of Chanukah arrives, bringing light and inspiration to Jews everywhere and we remember the miracle that took place 2000 years ago. And we give thanks.

CHRISTMAS EVE
By Bob Lockwood

The carols of Christmas never cease

To bring the hope of lasting peace,

Throughout the world this Holy Eve,

Whatever men in Christ believe,

The joyful strains bring back to them

The miracle of Bethlehem.

Tonight, as on that night gone by

When shepherds watched the Eastern sky

And guided by a brilliant star

Three Wiseman raveled from afar

In tribute of the Savior's birth

A solemn stillness cloaks the earth.

The spirit of this sacred night

Pervades each household with its light

Bringing to the hearthside scene

A sense of bliss and peach serene

As caught up in the mystic spell

The feeling comes that all is well.

CHRISTMAS LIST 1982
By Mary Reeves

WHAT I WANT:

- ◆ A two week paid vacation in a self contained motor home

- ◆ A complete new wardrobe costing at least $2000

- ◆ The strength and money to go on a diet, get a new hairdo, have a facial, manicure and pedicure

- ◆ A complete cooking course by Helen Corbitt, at Neiman's.

- ◆ A new house in the country, on five acres near a nice town, & all new furniture

- ◆ Early retirement

WHAT I DESERVE

- ◆ A month's cruise on the Queen Mary.

- ◆ A round trip to Paris with a letter of credit to all the fashion houses on Rue St. Honore.

- ◆ A month's stay at Neiman's Greenville (and a face lift)

- ◆ A maid to take a cooking course by Helen Corbitt

- ◆ 1600 Pennsylvania Ave.

- ◆ Early retirement with independent wealth

DESERT NIGHT
By Stella Klepac

The stars surpass themselves tonight;

The moon is shining marvelous bright.

The sky's a glittering wonder

Of dark and silver splendor.

All day-sounds one by one have ceased;

Our world is wrapped in wondrous peace.

The air is nectar, cool and sweet;

Earth and Heaven seem to meet…

Oh hush…be still…keep listening…

I thought I heard an angel sing!

DREAMING
By Toni Smith

What if we collected all that we've heard from the media, radio, town meetings, etc., all we have read in newspapers and magazines and information stuffed in our mail boxes; plus what we will be the recipients of in the months ahead and dump it all into a recycle bin for those who look for truth in trash.

Could we begin anew and build upward and outward on "Love Thy Neighbor as thyself?" This would not be a new concept, but one we know has merit in our world of diversity. True, it would not happen easily, (nor immediately,) but who says "easy" is the way good things always occur. Could this dream become reality? "DREAMING" certainly is much easier!

This was written several years ago during a campaign. However, not much has changed. If anything, circumstances have increased our insecurity, and our "worry button" is under constant pressure. We must remain alert and aware and make "Love Thy Neighbor" a reality, not just a DREAM!

EMBLEM OF LIBERTY
By Bob Lockwood

What Flag is this that floats on high,

Its colors bright against the sky

With broad and flaring stripes that yield

To white stars on a bright blue field

You're the emblem of my liberty

And great the hold you have on me.

Thought but a cloth of varied hue

I know your meaning through and through.

Justice, honor and faith all breathe

In every fiber of our weave.

Oh mark and standard of the free,

How great the hold you have on me.

In spite of doubts, in spite of fears,

Wave on triumphant through the years

Within your billowing folds embrace

The conscience of the human race

And backed by freedom's awesome might

Cast in our fate with truth and right.

IN RETROSPECT
By Bob Lockwood

Time gives to the warrior's stance

The golden luster of romance

While on the body, bent with pain,

Over the numbed and shattered brain,

Slowly, seeking to make amends,

The veil of history descends.

END OF THE RAINBOW?
An Ethereal poem by Frances McCreadie
Once
I saw
A rainbow
High in the sky
And reaching both ends
Holding a pot of gold
Tied to the earth with color
Opalescent hues shimmering
The message given to us is clear
A rainbow can be seen just when it's here!

Charles Stone—The Cockatiel

FREEDOM FLAG
By Marion Brown

Long gone
The men who forged our liberty
But their shining deed live on
Hearts swell with pride
At sight of our flag
Each star a tale
Told in history's lore
Of men who fought
For the rights of all
To be free
And to live in harmony
Always a reminder
Of how dear the cost
Paid for these rights
Our flag waves proudly
For all to see
Forever a symbol
Of the land of the free

GIVING
By Alvin Brewer

We are an echo seeking our source—
The closer we come, the clearer the sound.

We are light seeking our source—
The closer we come, the brighter the reflection.

We are the loved seeking our Lover—
The closer we come, the more loving we are.

Echoing, reflecting, loving—
But our truth is not in the degree of closeness.

It is in whether we will echo, reflect and love.
"For in loving we are loved,"
"In giving you receive."

Charles Stone—Safe Landing

GIVING THANKS AND WHY WE SHOULD
By George Gardiner

Each year in America much to do is made over Thanksgiving Day. On the last Thursday of November, families often travel great distances to be together. Mother or Grandmother spends long hours preparing a supreme meal; usually roast turkey with all the trimmings, topped off with pumpkin or mince pie. They visit, eat, nap, exchange hugs and words of affection, and then part again, often for another year.

Why do we do this? Is it because we have an annual craving for turkey? Or maybe a desire for a midweek day off to just loaf and watch a New York parade and endless football? Of course not.

The day of giving thanks has survived for many decades because men and woman of good faith sincerely desire to express gratitude and appreciation for a multitude of blessings that came to them with seemingly little effort on their part.

Each of us, in the depths of our being, knows that thanks is due to a power greater than we are, a power that most of us choose to call God. At least one day a year we want to pause, and in prayer, give thanks to Him whom we owe so much. We know we will feel better for it.

And, it is just the right thing, the comforting thing to do.

So, May God Bless Us, Each and Everyone, with a Happy and Grateful Thanksgiving Day!

INCIDENT AT THE TRAIN STATION
By Frances McCreadie

The long twilight of a summer evening was darkening around the old-fashioned railway station of this quiet western town. The last westbound train of the night had stopped briefly, discharged its passengers, and disappeared into the distance. The station was beginning to look deserted. My husband and I had just seen our eastern visitors safely aboard their home going train. Since moving from the east ourselves, we had come to enjoy the informality of western living and welcomed friends and relations who had always wanted to see the Rocky Mountains, Lake Louise and Banff. The station master, no longer a young man, was preparing to lock up for the night.

We wandered back into the building and found the station master talking in a foreign language to a shawl-wrapped person, holding a baby, with a shabby bundle at the person's feet. Clearly something was wrong. We moved closer and the station master told us the woman was to meet her husband but got off the train here instead of going to Lethridge one hundred miles west.

"There is no other train until morning," he told the woman. He checked her ticket through, which was in order, and reached for the phone to call the Lethridge station. My husband looked at me. I nodded.

"Wait," he said, "tell them we will look after her and the baby for the night and bring them back to catch the morning train so the husband can meet her at Lethridge." Explanations and arrangements were quickly made. We watched the frightened expression on her face relax a little. The station master relaxed, too, locked up and went home.

We all packed into the small car with baby and bundle. Baby was restless but we supplied milk and food as soon as we got home. Mother took over, and the little one was soon asleep in the quiet room. We all had a light meal and retired early.

Everyone woke up early and after breakfast, bundled into the car again. As we waited for the morning train to depart, the lady, looking younger than I thought the night before, tried to express her thanks. There is some kind of communication between people which transcends language barriers. I tried to tell her favors should not be returned, that is a dead end. Rather, try to pass it on to someone else in need so that an unbroken chain of help may reach farther than we can ever know. I think she understood.

I'D RATHER
By Aileen S. Mercurio

I'd rather be lost in a daisy field,
With the wind and the sun on my face,
Than be draped with jewels of silver and gold,
And be dressed in satin and lace.

I'd rather run free on a country road,
With the smell of cut hay on the air,
Than walk with the crowd on a city street,
And spend in the market there.

I'd rather sit quiet on a riverbank,
And eat from a brown paper sack,
Than be served at a table set with crystal and cloth,
While the man in the street suffers lack.

I can find joy in a shady place,
And I can bring sunshine there,
Where I can give comfort and bind up a hurt,
Sing a song, share a smile, say a prayer.

It's not what I take that fills up my cup,
It's what I can give away.
I'd rather be poor from sharing my love,
Than live a rich, selfish day.

LET THERE BE LIGHT!
By Toni Smith

Years ago on a typical New England Christmas Eve, we were celebrating our wedding anniversary with our family. A light snow had fallen, temperature moderately cold, and chimneys swirled smoke from fireplaces up into the sky. From where we sat in the dining room of the original home of a famous New Englander, now a popular restaurant, we could see lighted candles shining in every window. A huge decorated pine tree twinkled and sparkled in the foyer and smaller trees twinkled throughout the restaurant. The smell of pine wafted through the air accompanied by the aroma of a variety of foods. Our family of seven, three girls, two boys, Ralph and I were all clustered around a circular table enjoying a sumptuous meal. It took some time for all of us to be served, eat, and for decisions to be made over which dessert to choose. I could tell the boys were becoming restless.

"Can Lee and I walk around and look at the Christmas trees? We won't get lost, honest," asked Rick the eight year old. Ralph and I agreed knowing they couldn't go very far, and hoping both were on their good behavior. The girls sighed with relief. A short time later our desserts arrived, but the boys were nowhere in sight. As the boys" ice cream and chocolate sauce began to melt and puddle in the fancy dishes, we became anxious about our adventurers. Ralph got up to start looking when the two boys came swaggering up to the table their faces wreathed in smiles. There was something different about their appearance. Ah, ha! Both boys" suit coat pockets were bulging and they were clutching something in each hand.

"Oh no!" groaned our oldest daughter Nancy. "What have they done now?" Trying not to attract the attention of other diners, we checked their pockets. To our chagrin Rick and Lee had removed all the burned our Christmas tree light bulbs from the trees around the dining room. Their efforts must have been subtle and unobtrusive because no one was following them. The girls were horrified and embarrassed.

" I wanna go home," Cheryl the youngest wailed as tears trickled down onto her red velvet dress.

Ralph forced a smile on his face and motioned to our waiter. The girls covered their ears and bent their heads as far as possible. After a whispered conversation the boys followed behind the waiter like toy soldiers, and Ralph not far behind. I motioned to the girls and we joined the parade. As we reached the foyer we could see the head waiter engrossed in deep conversation with the two boys.

"We wish to thank you boys for your help in removing all these burned out bulbs. Here are the replacements. This young man will help you put them in the right places. When you get tired just say so and we will see that the job gets finished." He then turned to the girls and handed each one a small square box wrapped in red paper with a green bow. His gifts were accepted with weak smiles and a whispered thank you. The tall young man took each boy by the hand as they walked toward the huge tree in the foyer. We all watched silently. A couple passing by on their way out of the restaurant said "You have quite an unusual family."

When we left the restaurant the head waiter waved goodbye, wishing us, "Merry Christmas" Ralph and I smiled, "Merry Christmas."

LADY LIBERTY
By Marion Brown

Tall and regal
   There you stand
   Symbol of a cherished land
Your flame held high
   For all to see
   Your constant vigil
   O'er the Land of the Free.
You brighten the paths
   Into their "New World" entrée
   And give solace to all
   who approach your shores.
Your light always
   Beams out the truth
   Of the ideal held
   Within each man's soul
   Forever symbolizing
   The freedom of all
   To come and live
   Its promise true.
As you hold
   Your torch high
   Through generations of time
   Nothing can ever
   Diminish your light
     Lady Liberty.

MEMORIAL DAY
By Marion Brown

Long gone our heroes
Kept alive in memory
Of men who fought side by side
To preserve our freedoms,
One day each year flags unfurl
And medals gleam on display
As veterans march in parades
Across our nation.
Tales are told of battles fought
In far away lands,
Won by heroes who gave their lives
Forever asleep in foreign graves.
Now new generations of young men
And women too go forth,
Repeating war's scenario,
And our veteran's prayers
Go with them.
While PEACE waits patiently
Again in mourning
As TAPS echo across
Heroes' graves.

NOVEMBER DAYS
By Victoria Franks

Branches are leafless against the sky.

Snowflakes will soon be drifting by

Telling us winter is on the way.

Making us wish for an old fashioned sleigh.

It was such fun to go sledding outdoors

With wool caps, mittens and blanket galore.

Those galoshes bucked on our feet

Getting pushed down a hill, a special treat.

November days now, we all can recall

The brisk air, the squirrels who knew it was fall.

Thanksgiving is coming and time to say

Our thanks to the Lord, each and every day.

OVERFLOW
By Toni Smith

Let me not fret about what might have been

Nor what is going to be,

Nor fuss about what I have not

Nor what I cannot see.

Instead let me strive heartedly every day

To live each moment to the hilt—

And not to worry about what from my cup has spilled.

RANDOM THOUGHTS
By Rosemary Sample

Why do the best ideas come at the most inconvenient times? When listening to a sermon? When one is in the shower? When reading a non-fiction book that is supposed to have a message? When listening to a friends" long and sad complaint?

Living in a Senior Apartment complex is like High School without the raging hormones. There are hormones, but they are certainly not raging. The girls gather at mealtime and the gossip is about the latest news on TV and who moved in next door. There are a few boys and it's nice. Most of them get a second glance, but the best ones are already taken.

The golden years may be tarnished, for many of us so called "Recycled Teenagers", but when the sun is shining and our thought are matching the sun, life is good. We are right with God and still on the right side of the lawn.

SAFE HARBORS
By Alvin Brewer

On the journey of life,
When the sun shines bright,
And the winds blow steady,
 Sails are set to travel aright.

When the sky is dark,
And the seas are heaving,
The ships" dogs bark.
Safety, we're not leaving.

Our Guidance tells us to
Sail when all is ready,
And to drop the anchor
When the gale is unsteady.

Good sailors trust the Guidance,
When to come and when to go.
With the sails full of hope and
The anchors of faith in tow.

So, on with the journey of life.

SEPTEMBER 11TH, 2001
By Marion Brown

We took it all for granted,
Now it's like a lovely dream
Of "Once upon a time".
There was a land
Where freedom dwelt,
And spread her mantle
over one and all";
And we were safe
Within our shores.
Now we look askance
At the carnage wrought,
On a once proud city
Of world renown,
In deep mourning-
And our country weeps.
Thoughts of people
Were murdered here.
Now hallowed ground
Stands as monument of remembrance,
Always alive in our hearts and minds.
Our world will never be the same again,
We are mourning, but not bowed;
No longer placid.
We're like the Phoenix-
Rising from the ashes,
Fierce in our resurgence,
Guarding the blessings
       Of our precious freedoms
       And our shores.

SISTERS IN CHRIST
By Ellen Canterbury

We worshipped together

She and I

She held the hymnal

Her gnarled care-worn hands

Spoke of the years of labor

In the harsh land of the Navajos.

We sang together

She in Navajo,

I, in Finnish

We smiled

We were one

SUPPOSE
By Frances McCreadie

Suppose a child had not been born

Upon that early Christmas morn,

Suppose his mother Mary, mild,

Had never held the Holy child,

Suppose the wise men, traveling afar

Under the ever-guiding star,

Had never found the Babe who lay

Within a manger on the hay,

Suppose the angels" "Peace on Earth"

Had never proclaimed the Savior's birth.

Were all of these "supposes" true

Say, what would Christmas mean to you?

THANKFUL
By Iris Zukowski

It's a beautiful day in the neighborhood as Mr. Roger's would say. The colors of autumn are approaching a beautiful peak. The air is fresh and clear; as Pippa might say: "God's in heaven and all is well on our hilltop." This is the kind of day that one wants to say thanks for everything.

If this sounds like the beginning of my Thanksgiving Reflection, you are correct. I usually offer thanks for big things like sun and stars, our Earth. This year I've been thinking how many small things are around us that usually pass unnoticed. My friends usually tease me about liking really small things like the tiny teddy bear sitting on my phone now. But the small things do give praise by being small. And so, I offer thanks for all the little things that we probably don't think about very much.

What would we do without buttons, snaps, zippers and Velcro? What about plastic bags, Teflon, automatic coffee makers and TV remotes? Let us give thanks for these small conveniences. What about worms and microbes? They keep the soil healthy for every sort of veggie, flower (even dandelions) and tree. What about Bees and ants? They live in well-ordered communities, each fulfilling a purpose. There are butterflies and bird who, while adding beauty, perform the life perpetuating act of pollination. And what about the life substance DNA that makes us who we are? The same, but different as day and night. Let us offer thanks for each of these small but powerful wonders of nature.

What about all those switch, knobs and keys that make things work for us. Do we think about electron streams in tiny wires that obey the switches and knobs?

What about the chemical forces that hold salt and sugar crystals together and yet dissolve at our command? What about the air around us countless molecules and atoms all mixed together that we cannot see but cannot live without? How often do we think about water, hydrogen and oxygen -powerful alone- life sustaining together. Let us offer thanks for the magical stuff we call matter and energy.

Let us give thanks to our Creator for all these things in our lives; each doing its appointed task. Let us also give thanks for all the people who journey with us through all these wonders.

THE BREAK OF DAY
By Alvin Brewer

The darkness gradually yields to light.
The owl closes its eyes and takes its rest.
Other birds leave the comfort of their nest
And eagerly take to flight.

The sun peaks over the mountain top
And sheds its rays upon a new day.
Like the first dawning, the waters
Once shrouded in darkness, now sparkle
With the sun's gift.

While in parts of the earth, people sleep,
Here they awaken to the new dawning.
The routine of life begins again,
But never where it ended the night before.

This is a new day calling forth in us
That which is ever new.
Each moment in each heart beat,
We again practice life.

The sun calls out, "Accept my gift, love it,
Use it well and bless it as it blesses you.
For like this day, you are meant to break
Radiant with Joy.

THE MAGIC OF MUSIC
By Toni Smith

On a hot, cloudless summer afternoon Bob and I, two members of our combo, "the Half Notes", drove through town, and turned down on to a gravel road up to an adobe covered house. A sign on a painted wooden post at the road's entrance read "Desert Rest." Bob drove the truck up the driveway and parked close to the front entrance. Almost hidden by a large mesquite tree, I became concerned about how small the house looked. Would we find enough room to set up our equipment? This was our first time playing for residents of an assisted-living facility housed in a former private home.

Bob went around to the back of the pick-up truck and began unloading our instruments. I carried my keyboard case in one hand, music stand in other and walked to the door. Bob followed with his drums and amp. I reached the front door and rang the door bell. It took some time before an attractive young woman opened the door. "Oh, no." I thought. "Did we have the wrong day?"

"Oh, I am so glad to see you. We were worried that the heat might keep you away." She was dabbing at her face with a towel. "We have been talking to the residents for days about your visit." She turned and motioned for us to follow her.

"My name is Inez, and I am the Supervisor for "Desert Rest". I am so sorry, but our air conditioning has broken down, and the maintenance man has not been here as yet. Follow me." We followed Inez through a large dining room and into a small living room.

"Make yourself at home. Set up where ever it is convenient for you, and we will fit our residents in around you."

We followed Inez into the small living room with over-stuffed chairs and a large sofa. Drapes had been drawn over the windows to keep out the heat from the afternoon sun, and several lamps had been turned on which made the room seem smaller and warmer. Joe, our trumpet player, had followed a few minutes behind us and was soon helping to set up our equipment. Joe and Bob tucked the drums in between the two overstuffed chairs. I squeezed my keyboard and amp in beside the drums, and Joe stood close to a big rubber tree plant which looked ready to pick his back pocket. Our equipment was all set up, and we were ready to begin. The heat was stifling. I wished I had brought my bottle of water, but had been afraid I would be late if I had gone back inside the house for it when Bob picked me up.

Joe was ready to begin his introduction when a male voice beside him said, "Excuse me, I am Jim, a caregiver here and I will need a little more room for this wheelchair. Hope it won't be in your way."
"You will be fine here, Delia," Jim said looking down at a tiny beautifully dressed lady in the wheelchair. He patted her hand which lay limp on the arm of her chair. "Do not worry, I will be right back." He turned to us and said softly, "We do not know why, but she cannot move without help, nor does she speak. She is not blind, but does not appear to see, however, I believe Delia is aware of her surroundings."

Inez brought in the other residents some of whom could walk by themselves and others needed walkers or canes. The room was crowded with people, furniture, musical equipment, and the heat was oppressive. Yet, the residents looked at us with smiles of anticipation. Trickles of perspiration ran down the back of my neck, Bob wiped his brow, and Joe wiped his fingers so they would not stick to the trumpet keys.

We were ready, Inez had served everyone a cold drink, and the buzz between the residents had ceased. Joe looked at the expectant audience and gave the introduction.

"Good afternoon, I am Joe, on trumpet, Toni on keyboard, Bob on Drums, and we are the Half-notes. We will play good old swing tunes of the thirties and forties, and some sing along tunes. This music is for you to join with us by singing, clapping or even dancing if you so desire."
When Joe mentioned dancing, several people looked at one another, smiled and shook their heads.

We opened our program with "There Are Smiles That Make You Happy," One or two of the residents began humming, and soon others joined by singing. We could feel the change in the room. People relaxed. Ache and pains were forgotten as memories of happier times surfaced and smiles shone on the faces around the room. I became mesmerized with the lady in the wheelchair, Delia. She was truly beautiful. Her complexion was without a wrinkle; however her face was expressionless, her blue eyes blank and her mouth, though expertly painted, drooped at the corners. Sadness seemed to envelope her whole body. Lifeless. It was as if she were in another world. Jim sat beside her while we played the first song. She did not show any signs of movement. Nothing seemed to register.

When we began playing, "Moon Glow," Jim reached down, took her small immobile hands in his and gently began to pull her forward. He carefully lifted her out of the wheel chair into his arms. Her body was limp and her tiny legs and feet dangled like a puppet's. All eyes became riveted on these two people. Slowly Jim with Delia, moved into the small space in the middle of the room and began swaying to the music. Delia's face began to slowly change before our eyes as if awakening from a long nap. The corners of her mouth lost their droopiness and began to curve into a smile. I looked at her eyes and there was brightness not noticeable before.

We were all spellbound. As Jim held her, and moved in time with the music, her body seemed to move closer, and her hand on his shoulder seemed to move so that her fingers curved to fit his shoulder. A tenor voice from the back of the room began singing softly the words to "Moon Glow". A radiant smile broke over Delia's face and she began to respond to Jim's dance movements. Her body appeared to come to life and her hands clung to him. Jim watched her in amazement and held her as if she were the most important person in the world.

As I glanced around the room, tears were trickling down some of the resident's cheeks. We kept on playing, struggling with our own emotions. We glanced at one another. We did not know whether to stop playing, or let the miracle play out to its finish. It was decided for us. The background voice slowly faded away, and we followed the lead. Jim slowed his movements and began to move Delia toward her wheelchair. All was quiet.

As Delia was slowly lowered into her chair, the light slowly disappeared from her eyes. Jim carefully placed her listless hands in her lap. While we watched, Delia slowly slipped back into the world she alone knew. The smile faded, the body became rigid, but her eyes were moist and a tear slid slowly down her cheek.

We will always remember beautiful Delia in the dimly lit living room of "Desert Rest" who shared for a few moments, a part of our world, and then slipped quietly back into her own. We shall never forget Delia, and how we felt sharing her Magic Moment.

THE RIGHT WORDS AT THE RIGHT TIME
By Mary Reeves

It was early in 1954 when I found myself alone with my 6 year old son. My husband of one year had been sent to France for 18 months by the Air Force.

I was 27 years old and working, even had family nearby, but still I became very lonely and on the verge of depression. I had been prone to depression all my life in spite of Mother telling me to "straighten up".

I realized I needed help and went to a Doctor I had never met before, sure he would give me some sort of magic pill. After hearing my sad tale and a complete physical he said: "There is nothing wrong with you—you just need to get up and out. Take your child to church—it will help you."

It was the right time for me to hear these words, which initially angered and shocked me! In my heart I knew I had been emotionally neglecting my son, and sure it would help to have God on my side, I did exactly what the Doctor advised and soon found a really friendly wonderful church, and made friends there. I began to enjoy life.

Since that experience more than 50 years ago I have had low times and always remembered what the Doctor said and how I was helped. Now I try to reach out, get up, get out and find happiness!

THE WILD BLUE YONDER
By Frances McCreadie

In 1939, when England declared war against Germany's invasion of European countries, Canada and Australia quickly followed. My brother, Roy, was 16. Three years later he was in the Royal Canadian Air Force, had earned his Pilot Officer's wings, and was flying in the European theater.

Bill and I had just built our first home, had two small children, a dog and a mortgage. Life was fairly simple until Bill began to feel patriotic. He should enlist, his country needed him. He would offer his services to the R.C.A.F. He had always wanted to learn to fly. Now the government would teach him and pay him as well. Here was the opportunity. As for the recruiting officer, he was eager to accept an accountant with mathematical skills and a high I.Q. Bill was assured they would do all they could to assign him to a nearby post so he could frequently have weekend passes home while in training. Off he went, amid tears and cheers of the family, to Toronto manning depot and within twenty four hours was sent across country to Edmonton Alberta, for basic training.

The next two years were a succession of transfers from one western training center to another – Edmonton, Calgary, Vulcan, High River, McLeod and finally, for navigational flight training to Winnipeg which was, at least, one thousand miles closer to home. But that was only half way. During one precious leave, when he managed the long two thousand mile journey for one short week at home, I asked if he had to train for parachute jumping. It seemed a logical question. He gave me a slightly exasperated, half amused, tolerant and totally superior look husbands assume when they feel completely and absolutely correct.

"Dear one," he said, and repeated it for emphasis. "I pack my own parachute so I am wholly responsible. I sit on the parachute during flight. If I have to jump, buckled up I am out the door. The parachute should open. If it works, fine; if not I won't need anymore training." Happily, my husband finished his training in good health.

At the end of the war my brother and his crew barely managed the ocean flight to Canada in their war battered plane that was scarcely capable of flying. But I am thankful to report the war ended for me with the safe return of all my friends and loved ones.

TO CLIMB A RAINBOW (The farewell of a Siamese Cat)
By George Gardiner

We knew about things, you and me,
The windy braches high in a tree
Sleeping curled on a quilted bed,
And the secret things the hummingbird said.

We slept in a pool of warm sunlight,
And dreamed of things to do at night
And secret places we two could meet,
Around the corner and down the street.

We've hid together to watch a storm,
And climbed a wall when the night was warm,
We've played with stars that fell too low,
And smeared our cheeks with sunset glow.

When I came to you each dawn,
You'd smile at me then we would yawn,
Then before the day would start,
I'd leave my paw prints on your heart.

We've had a honeysuckle love affair,
I think we've been a queenly pair
We learned to laugh and love and play,
But now I've loved my life away.

Don't let the roses hear you cry,
I climbed a rainbow, I didn't die.
When the moon is low look for me,
Playing in our Chinaberry Tree.

Remember how I loved to sleep?
Remembering then why do you weep?
I'll roll in star dust and wash in rain,
Till someday when we'll play again.

TUCSONANS LOVE THE RAIN By Stella Klepac

Our rain is not a piddling rain,
Our rain in Arizona.
It does not come by sneak and
stealth,

Not in a gentle drizzle,
Nor yet a quiet downpour,
Like the rains of the Northland.

It comes—proudly announced
By low and sooty black clouds,
Hugging the mountains.
They grow into big, black fists,
Surging and charging into
town—
Into Tucson, begging for rain.

It comes in noisy sheets,
It descends and swoops in
frenzied showers,
Whipped by the wind,
Slamming against the houses,
Shivering against the windows,
Lashing the trees.

People watch—
And in fancy feel the cool water
Pouring over them.

It comes with mighty
orchestration,
Ear-splitting cymbal clangs,
Drum rolls in endless fermata,
With sky-filling fireworks
A blitzkrieg, indeed!

People watch—
Astounded—
Though they have seen it before.

It rivers along the streets
And leaps into the arroyos.

Great barren ditches, called
Santa Cruz, Rillito, Pantano,
Great barren ditches
Become murderous ranging tor-
rents.

It flows along the desert floor,
And all the thirsty desert plants,
And all the thirsty desert
creatures
Drink their fill.

It is welcomed,
It is thrice welcomed…
Tucsonans love the rain.

WHERE IS CHRISTMAS?
By Ellen Canterbury

It seemed inconceivable to me, that I, a winter snow-dweller, would find the desert my home. What of Christmas? Sleigh bell, icicles, and snow? Trees laden with ermine cloaks and the squeaky frost of freezing night? Where could the spirit of Christmas dwell except in the warmth of a fireplace after a day's trek to choose the best spruce tree on forty acres? Or, in the glow of children's faces returning fro hours spent romping in the snow?

Could I be wrong? I now live in a desert environment such as Jesus knew. Our Savior was born in a barren land. Shepherds watched the flocks under starlit skies where the stuffy growth was all for sheep to feed upon. Wooly cloaks sheltered the shepherds in their long night watches.

Jesus dwells in every place, in every heart, where the door is open to receive. Christmas comes as a daily gift. It is to the inner being that the light celestial brings it shattering glow of *LOVE*.

'TWAS THE NIGHT
By Toni Smith

" *'Twas the night before Christmas and all through the house...*"
It was seven o" clock and the wedding was at eight. My wedding! As I
struggled putting the vacuum in the broom closet, the front door bell
rang. I stumbled over the dust mop caught my balance, and opened the
door. "Aren't you dressed yet?" my future mother-in-law glanced at me
in horror. "Where are the flowers?"

A modest home wedding. No fuss. Nothing to it, everyone said.
Just a dress, some flowers, a cake, cookies and punch. No fancy invitation, just a note with an R.S.V.P. card enclosed. Yep, that's what everyone said, simple! Well let me tell you something; that ain't so! A simple
wedding is not simple. Without going into the boring details just let's
say, "Let the Wedding Begin," once I had my gown on of course.

My mother-in-law-to-be wrangled with the florist finally convinc-
ing them the wedding was that night, not the following week. The house
was as clean as it would get, and the refreshments were all ready except
for a few items which would arrive later with one of the guests now it
was off to be a bride!

I checked with my father who was trying not to strangle himself
with his tie. My sister, the teenage bridesmaid, was throwing a hissie
over trying to tie her sash in front and swishing it around to the back,
with little or no success. Me? I was worried about getting all those little
buttons up the back of my dress by looking in the mirror. I was
almost in tears. My head hurt from twisting around and trying to remember that everything was reversed in the mirror.

Suddenly a dear friend burst into the bedroom, took me by the
shoulders and said, "Let me help!" I did. When we heard the pianist began playing the wedding march, we knew it was time. I slowly started
the procession down the stairs for my "Simple" wedding.

As I reached the bottom of the stairs, I saw our special friend and
pastor waiting for me. He winked. (There were no visible signs of the
chicken pox from which he had just recuperated.) He took my hand,

and I stopped and stared in complete amazement. The living room was beautiful. There was the Christmas tree, the candles, the flowers, and all the smiling faces of friends and family. Best of all, the groom, the groom with his special smile. A simple wedding it was indeed. Sixty two years later I can still say, "It was simply wonderful!"

Bernice Steinhauser—Lillies

CHAPTER TWO

Birds Of A Feather

Having a common residence doesn't necessarily mean the Residents are common.

You'll find the most uncommon and interesting people here at Fellowship Square!

A SECRETARY'S TRAVEL TALE
By Robbie Robinson

Donaleta "Robbie" Robinson began her secretarial career with the Defense Department shortly after WWII. Robbie had owned a gift shop and rental library, and taught her self typing and shorthand during quiet times at the shop. After the war, Robbie worked at the San Francisco Port of Embarkation, starting in the typing pool, and then progressing to secretary for an Army Colonel. It was during this time she learned to take dictation. During the Korean War, Robbie gained further experience as secretary to the Director of Operations of the San Francisco Port of Embarkation when this Port was the main conduit for overseas troops and supplies.

Robbie transferred to the Pentagon, and began working in the Administrative Office of the Secretary of Defense, who at the time was Charles Wilson. Robbie and other staff members were considered part of the inner office and were often included in the parties given in the Secretary of Defense's private dinning room. One of her most memorable days at the Pentagon was when she was working as secretary to an Assistant General Counsel. All day she had typed and retyped questions and answers as dictated to her by her boss and Cyrus Vance, Chief Lawyer to the Secretary of Defense, for President Kennedy to use regarding the Little Rock crisis. It was a thrill to hear President Kennedy read on the evening news, what she had been typing all day.

Later in her career she transferred to the Air Force Inspector General's office, in San Bernardino, California. After four years Robbie and the Brigadier General for whom she was secretary were transferred to NATO headquarters in Paris, for the last year that NATO was in France. After NATO was moved to Brussels, Robbie was transferred to Wiesbaden, Germany to be a secretary to a Lt. General, who was Deputy Commander in Chief of the U.S. Air Forces in Europe. When the Lt. General to whom she was assigned received his fourth star, Robbie was urged to give up Europe and move back to the states. When she arrived at Wright-Patterson AFB in Ohio, she was dismayed to find a Colonel doing her job! Robbie resigned her position and accepted a job working once again in the Pentagon. After one year she returned to Germany, where she was accepted as secretary to a Deputy Commanding Officer at Army Headquarters in Germany. After five years in Germany, she rotated to Fort Huachuca in Arizona. Eighteen months later she retired, after thirty-three years with the defense department.

After retiring, she learned the Laubach method of teaching adults to read and write, to keep busy and help others. She recruited volunteers who were trained to become tutors for the adult students that had been referred to her through the Post Education Center. After three years of full time work, Robbie moved back to Europe with her cat, Whisky.

Fourteen years later, Robbie moved to Tucson. After a visit to her home near Cannes, Robbie hopes she doesn't get the yen to travel again.

Charles Stone—Flights Of Fancy

AN INTERESTING LADY
Interview by Toni Smith

Jeanine Surwit, at 15 years of age, came by herself to the United States, from France in 1938. Her brother left on the last children's transport in the early forties. It was imperative that they leave France, and it was a frightening experience. Her parents were in the Auschwitz concentration camp and Jeanine did not know if she would ever see them again. Jeanine settled in Staten Island, New York where she entered high school. She didn't know a word of English but through hard work and determination she finished the four year curriculum in two years. Her brother's trip to the U.S. was by way of North Africa taking six weeks, and he settled in Wilmington, Delaware.

Later a cousin, who lived in the Maryland suburbs of D.C., knew Jeanie was unhappy in New York, and suggested she move to Maryland, which she did. She was invited to a dance where the younger brother of her cousin introduced her to the man who would soon become her husband. After a three week courtship, they were married. Her husband was an accountant by profession. When he was inducted into the service he was assigned to the Army's 10th Armored Division Fighting Unit. Because of his accounting ability, he was later assigned to the paymaster's office in Marseilles, France, during the Battle of the Bulge. At that time Jeanine worked at the French Purchasing Department, and through the resources available, she learned that her parents had died in Auschwitz.

After the war, it was necessary that Jeanine continue working. She had always been interested in the medical field, so she found a job working with a urologist, and worked in this capacity for ten years. In the early 70"s, Jeanine volunteered her services as a tour guide for the Kennedy Center of the Performing Arts. She had many memorable experiences there, and her tour of duty lasted twenty years. One favorable experience was giving a tour to Jackie Kennedy. Jackie was an unaffected, gracious lady. "A REALLY nice lady," said Jeanine. She loved her job at the Center and watched many changes over the years.

Jeanine lost her husband several years ago and upon the suggestion of her son who resided here, came to Tucson to live. She made use of her medical background by volunteering at TMC where she worked in the orthopedic area helping people who had knee replacement surgery.

She has maintained a busy life with her many talents. Jeanine has made exquisite jewelry and beautiful, intricately knitted articles. Her collections are varied; bells, angels, clowns, miniature tea cups, to mention a few. She is a fascinating lady with many a story to tell.

Ann Mari Brandt—Still Life

AVA'S FULL TIME DEVOTION
Interview by Toni Smith

Ava June Wolf, a resident at Fellowship Square, was born in Hallettsville, Texas, ninety miles from Austin. She went through school and received a degree in Medicine. Her first contact with Native Americans was her lab partner in medical school, Taylor McKensie, the first Navajo M.D. This association had a meaningful effect on her future.

Pediatrics was her main interest at this time, and she was completing her first residency in Cleveland Ohio. While there, she joined with Russell Meane in starting an Native American Clinic, and this joint venture whetted her appetite for providing medical help to Native Americans, and started her on her journey to reach that goal. While in Cleveland she met a medical student who later became her husband; and in time they had four daughters. While her children were young, Ava was inactive in her career, but later went back to school for repeat training in pediatrics, in Oklahoma.

From Cleveland the next stop was Washington D.C. where she promoted a Group House. She met two Native American law students, one a Comanche and the other a Shawnee, and a strong friendship developed. Both felt that Ava should join the Native American Health Service; and these two men later gained prominence in their own tribes. Her desire to help Native Americans became the focal point of her career.

A once in a lifetime opportunity presented itself when she was hired with two other pediatricians to work in Chinle, Arizona, located on the Navajo reservation in the northern part of the state. Their job was to try to reduce the after-effects of meningitis and deafness from ear infections which were common on the reservation. Ava served as Director of medical education and developed a diabetes education program that was adopted by other service areas on the reservation. She was a contributor to a five-year health plan for a hospital on the central reservation. She spent the next five years from 1974-1978 with the Navajo, which were very productive and included establishing the hospital in Chinle; with the hospital being dedicated in 1979.

She respected the Navajo people, and had the opportunity to work with some of their medicine men and medicine women who were fascinating. The medicine women had to be older, beyond childbearing age, and full blooded Navajo. The opportunity to work with the Navajo was the most rewarding job of her life.

Her children have followed their mother's love of medicine. They have degrees in psychology and medicine. While here in Tucson, Ava trained two medical practitioners who then went to Chinle and lived in her former house on the reservation. She still keeps in contact with people she knew and worked with in Chinle. Ava has left a legacy that shows her devotion, and the fulfillment of her desire to help the Navajo people.

Charles Stone—Tucson Roadrunner

BILL'S UNPLANNED SOJOURN
Interview by Toni Smith

Bill Moore was a fighter pilot with the 8th Air Force, 399 Fighter Group during W.W. II, whose job was to escort bombers into Germany and later to strafe enemy planes on the ground. On September 13th, 1944 his plane was hit by flak which eventually caused his engine to quit, requiring him to bail out at high speed. He was knocked unconscious and regained consciousness hanging in a tree in his parachute harness about one hundred yards away from his burning plane. Finding himself in this position was not what Bill had in mind when he left the air field that morning. Three German farmers rescued him, took him to their farmhouse, called the police whereupon he became a "Kriegie", German terminology for prisoner of war.

With Luftwaffe officers in charge, he traveled across parts of Germany to interrogation centers, was in solitary confinement for a short time, and a train trip of four days with ten men to a compartment which normally seated six. Arriving at Barth, Germany, they were again searched and questioned. Before going to the compound, Stalag Luft #1, their clothes were deloused, and Red Cross parcels were given to them. This was home now, but for how long? No one knew!

October 20th, Bill began a journal to his wife on the back of a cigarette package, which was small and easy to hide. Every day, Bill would write a letter to his wife telling her of day's activities which followed the same routine for all thirteen internees in Bill's barracks. Reveille, outdoor roll call rain or shine, wind or snow. Breakfast always was a toasted cheese sandwich and coffee. After the morning chores were finished, it was time to prepare dinner which usually consisted of potatoes, cabbage, meat, toast, and coffee. Once in a while they had prunes, and occasionally a snack of some kind. All meals were cooked on the stove that heated the cabin, and dishes were cleaned with water hauled into the cabin. The menu seldom varied and seldom did the routine.

Laundry was a hardship, so did not rate a high priority. Cleaning and making beds happened only when necessary, especially when someone yelled. "Search party". That meant the "Gerries" were going to search the barracks. Wintertime was unpleasant because the stoves were not too efficient; the days were long, and monotonous. Bill made a cribbage board, and a few decks of cards had come as gifts in some of the Red Cross parcels. Everybody was lonesome and worried about their families. Without any outside contact they did not know if anyone knew if they were alive, let alone P.O.W.'s. Mail call was the biggest event, but it didn't occur too often. There were many bull sessions after lights out.

On October 22nd, Bill made an unhappy discovery; and wrote the following in his journal: "Gosh I am a dummy. Today is our wedding anniversary, six months ago today; two of which we were together and the rest separated."

So the days went on and on. Outside camp, the war was still going on, but they received no information as to who was winning. Christmas was hard, but they managed to have a celebration.

In February the Germans started talking about how the Russians were advancing. The winter was bitterly cold, but as spring approached the situation improved. By May, 1945 the prisoners realized the end was in sight after receiving news from the Germans and the outside world that the Russians were indeed advancing. On May 13, 1945, B17"s from the 8th Air Force started loading the internees from Stalag Luft #1, which ended Bill's unplanned sojourn. Now Bill could say "Goodbye you Gerries, I'm headed home!"

BLUE CEILING
Interview by Toni Smith

When Alberta Kinney left her home state of Montana to go to Seattle to find a job in 1944, little did she realize what direction her life would take. Her first job was with the Civil Service as a secretary in the Planning and Estimating department of the Navy. During this time she earned her private pilots license under the tutelage of an Alaskan bush pilot. In February of 1944, she decided to do her part in serving her country. The organization, WASP, Women Air Force Service Pilots, had been formed in 1943. The purpose of this organization was to free male pilots for overseas duty.

Having earned her private pilot's license, one of the requirements for the WASP, she decided to apply for training. She was accepted and entered seven months of rigorous training to earn her wings. The training program consisted of the same qualifications for women as for men. The units marched everywhere, had the same drill instructors, ate and worked the same details, wore fatigues, bought their own dress uniforms, and if they did not pass the tests they washed out just like the men. The purpose was proving that women could do what the men did under the same conditions to earn their wings. No favoritism was shown.

The WASP training was out of Victoria, Texas. Due to erratic weather patterns graduation did not occur as scheduled in July, but later. With graduation the women were given three choices. One, as a pilot they could match up with another pilot; two, fly a particular plane; or three, apply for a particular location in the U.S.A. Alberta choose number one. The WASP pilots flew every kind of plane from trainers to B-29"s. Full women crews on a multi engine aircraft were not uncommon. Alberta's assignment was to fly an AT6 towing a target sleeve behind the aircraft for aerial gunnery practice at a moving target. The WASP's were never commissioned as military pilots even though they were under military discipline and completed many tiring and hazardous missions. They Air Force pilots were glad the WASP's were there because that enabled them to fly overseas.

In December 1944 when male pilots came home in increasing numbers, the WASP disbanded. They had not received the military status they had been promised, but thirty four years later this omission was corrected. When the war was over, Alberta continued her love affair with flying. She taught ground school for the Air Force and later she trained Air Force pilots for civilian flying so they could get their commercial license.

After the war, Alberta and her husband traveled extensively, lived in different countries, and returned to the U.S.A. to settle in Gross Pointe, Michigan where they maintained a busy life. About her experience, Alberta said that she had a job she loved, and while doing what she enjoyed, could, and did serve her country. One of her fondest memories of flying was climbing into a plane, soaring upwards just before dusk to survey a magnificent sunset, and feeling the wonder of the beauty all around her.

I HAVE HAD A BLAST…
Interview by Toni Smith

…was Priscilla's answer when asked about her life. Although she was born in Massachusetts she lived in Europe for 33 years. Priscilla has had many interesting jobs and journeys, including marriages, in her life. These events were chronicled in an article in a Tucson paper and included her time working with the Red Cross in New Guinea during WWII. After she returned to the U.S. she took a job as a secretary for Scientific American Magazine.

One day she notified her boss that she was going to Ghana. Her boss was very surprised and asked her what prompted this decision. "To find my ancestral roots," was her explanation. She had learned that her grandfather was part Chinook Indian and part black and lived in Ghana. He came to America and became a slave. Priscilla's grandmother came from Scottish ancestry and owned slaves, including her grandfather. Her grandmother told her grandfather, Frank, his American name to -- "get in this buggy, we are leaving the South and going to Massachusetts to get married." At that point he became a run-away slave. He was frightened of what might happen, but nothing occurred to prevent the marriage. She looked forward to the trip to Ghana, and whatever else she would discover about her ancestors.

She lived in a beautiful four bedroom, three and a half bathroom, two story house which overlooked the ocean in Takaradi, which was not far from the capitol, Aruca. Her rent was $89 every thirty days. Priscilla wanted to get around and see places and people, but she did not have a car. So she asked Kofi, (so named because he was born on a Friday), to help her pick out a camel to purchase. Kofi was surprised. Did she really plan to ride this camel around town? The transaction was completed for the total amount of $20. The camel lived on the property and took care of trimming the grass and troublesome weeds.

One day Priscilla was invited by Awuku, chief of a local tribe, to visit a village where he was going to settle a dispute. "Adjoa," Priscilla's Ghana name, "I believe I know the village where your grandfather lived. Do you want to go there?"

She replied that she would like that very much. There she found what she had waited so long to know about her family. Although there are 83 dialects in Ghana, she learned how to converse with the people and lived very happily there for four years.

She has presented 12 sets of bronze busts of famous black Americans to more than a dozen Universities in an effort to strengthen understanding between the two countries. She came to Arizona for her health, but remained active for many years. She served as surrogate mother to 22 Malaysian students at the "U" of Arizona and later visited Malaysia. Yes, I think we would agree when she says with her wonderful smile, "I have had a blast."

Charles Stone—Rose Vase

LOVABLE "D's"
Interview by Toni Smith

The mystery and awe surrounding dinosaurs and Jurassic Park is not dead. You can see a modern day dinosaur in a comfortable environment by taking a walk around our complex. Staring out the window of Phyllis Amos" apartment are six dinosaurs, completely dressed, including scuba diving gear, ready for a trip to Hawaii. They are generic, but true to their genealogy in color and physical structure. Phyllis calls them her "kids" and gives them TLC.

The arrival of these creatures is very mysterious. They just appeared, didn't want to leave, so she adopted each one, giving them a safe and secure shelter. It was obvious from early on that each had a definite personality. T-Rex (Tyrannosaurus), was the first. He appointed himself the Boss because he was the biggest. T-Rex had only to thump his tail once and all knew he was BOSS. Spike is from Colorado (Stegosaurus), and is by nature a lover. Fred from Montana, (Triceratops) is a chronic complainer. Little One from France, (Brontosaurus) became the peacemaker. The word's out! The dinosaur Oasis is here! Elmer from Mongolia, (Velociraptor) is the Jokester. He and Dudley, a Wooly Mammoth from Siberia, were the last to take up residence. Their varied backgrounds and diverse personalities have blended into an unusually compatible dinosaur community. Flying overhead, like a watchful helicopter, is Lindy (Pterodactyl) who has flown around the world and is still flying. Tarzana, who resides in the back closet because she prefers solitude, wears Tarzan-type clothes, and is really dynamite in a small package. She helps Phyllis keep this group under control, and is respected in this dinosaur community.

These "kids" are in tune with our world and celebrate our holidays, participate in important activities, and keep physically fit. There are moments of discontent, when Fred complained about his Hawaiian outfit, but Peacemaker stepped in and calmed the waters. The atmosphere is relaxed.

Phyllis led a busy life working in the Administrative field until she retired. She has volunteered as a storyteller to children in hospitals and other facilities. The Salvation Army was one of her favorite volunteer jobs. The bell ringing gave her great satisfactions. She enjoyed her life and her "kids". (I wonder if she ever fed them any of her Peanut Butter Fudge? Oh, but that is a whole different story.) The dinosaurs have brought new friends and discoveries, and she lets us enjoy these little refugees from Jurassic Park as we walk by her window. Who says dinosaurs are not lovable? Watch for new friends, you never know who or what they might be.

Charles Stone—The Mallards

MEMORIES OF MIRIAM LEVITAN SPECTOR
Interviewed by Toni Smith

An influential cousin successfully moved Miriam's family from Russia to Palestine. When they arrived, having hired a horse and buggy and purchased a tent, he brought the family from Jaffa across the desert to Nes Ziona. The trip across the desert was unusual because all that could be heard were the cries of the jackals, and there were no lights except from a Jewish Boys School near Rishon Le Zion. Where they pitched their tent in the desert sands is now Tel Aviv. Miriam was born in Rishon Le Zion, a town near Nes Ziona, where her grandparents had lived. She remembers an incident when she was three years old, riding a donkey, falling off, and having a bruise on her forehead that left a scar in the shape of the number 7. The donkey and camel were the only means of transportation at that time.

When she was five years old her family left Israel, and came to the United States by way of Canada. They would save enough money in America so that in time they could return to Israel, buy land and plant an orange grove. The family settled in Chicago Ill., where her father became a fine cabinetmaker, and also worked at a museum. Miriam attended grade school, high school and college in Chicago. She also received a thorough Yiddish education at the Maccabe Folk School and sang in their advanced choir, doing some solos. She maintained that interest during her life and has always sung in some choir. Miriam loves reading and corresponding in Yiddish, which comes from a background of absorbing the writings of great Yiddish literature.

Miriam and Sam Spector were sweethearts for five years. He proposed marriage at 23, and although she could not leave her widowed mother with her younger sister at 12 and an eight-year-old brother, he said he would still marry her. Sam moved in with the family and had Miriam's mother quit her job so that she could take care of the family. The family has grown over the years, Sam and Miriam had three children, along with grandchildren and great grandchildren.

During their marriage, Sam and Miriam traveled to many wonderful places, including five trips to Israel, where they enjoyed seeing the changes each visit. There were trips to England, Italy, France, Switzerland and Norway that were exciting. Cruises to Alaska, Hawaii, and the Philippines were wonderful. "Our children have always been our joy," writes Miriam in her memoirs. In 1977, ten days before his 95th birthday Sam passed away. Miriam has continued her traveling and singing, including starting the Villa Voices Chorus group at Fellowship Square, who perform annually in and around the community. Miriam also keeps physically fit with swimming and chair exercise, leading a group at Fellowship Square each week.

Miriam celebrated her 100th birthday in 2006.

MEET THE BREWERS'
By Alvin Brewer

Rosella and Alvin have been residents since June 2004, when they moved from Green Valley following their marriage. Prior to living in Green Valley, Rosella, who is a native of Montana, lived with her late husband, Vern, for 23 years in Alaska; where she raised her son, nursed her ill husband and had an interesting career in Education. Following the marriage of two grown daughters, she pursued a course of learning which led to a Ph. D in Recent Relevant Brain Research and its implications to learning, centering upon The Lozanov Method which in this country is called Super Learning. She published three books for teachers in elementary education, (a field in which she had practiced).

She became a professor at the University of Alaska, supervising student teachers. Under a special grant, she traveled throughout Alaska working with Native Elders on a project to help preserve their languages; often spending two or more weeks at remote sites. She continues a lifelong interest in spiritual growth, the latest developments in brain research, and the implications of quantum physics to both.

Alvin and his late wife Carol moved to Green Valley following his retirement from the ministry of the United Church of Christ, in which Alvin served churches in Michigan, Connecticut, New York City and North Carolina. He has three sons living outside of Arizona and a daughter in Tucson. He shares with Rosella a lifelong interest in avenues of spiritual development, including a study of metaphysics. He is preparing to publish a compilation of poetry, (a few of which are included in this volume). Rosella has also composed many poems, and we include one here to reflect our feelings about describing one's self by "what you did".

WHAT WERE YOU?
By Rosella Brewer

What did you do?
What was your profession or work?
What did you do?
Did you do housework or clerk?
What was your aspiration?
What was your job or employment?
What was your passion?
Was it a source of enjoyment?

Hey, let's skip the past tense questions.
No need for this third degree.
My job is to be healthy
As I work on a happiness Ph.D.
It matters little what I did before,
I'm living right here and now.
I'm still growing and evolving,
That's all that counts anyhow.

SOMETHING VERY SPECIAL SMOOTH—NICE AND HOT!
Freshly Brewed And Poured Directly From the Pot
(That pours two cups at once!) By Toni Smith

And that is not all! Scrumptious goodies, warm hospitality, and a welcome not soon forgot!

Yes siree, at Maradine's Coffee Shop. "The Best Coffee in Town," the little sign says. Maradine moved here in 2004 and immediately set up her coffee shop. This was not a new idea but a continuation of what she had been doing wherever she lived. "Why?" You might ask. Her answer, "Because I like to do it". Her first guests here were invited by a "Y"all come" type of invitation. Now the coffee hour is posted on a sign hanging by her front door—date and time. Those in the know keep careful watch.

This is no ordinary shop, as the "faithful will gladly tell you". She has tried many different kinds of coffee, and still experiments with new flavors, but keeps the good ole brands on hand. If you prefer tea, just ask and she probably has most flavors you might request. Espresso, yes, her special mix. "But is it just coffee?" you ask. No, much more.

She has offered a warm friendly atmosphere which wraps around one like a fuzzy blanket. There is laughter along with engaging conversation, and time is of no importance—there is no time limit to the flow of coffee or conviviality.

Maradine can relate some very interesting stories about her coffee "shops". One time, the "grind and brew" became totally confused and decorated her kitchen with coffee grounds which did not blend well with her décor.

Did you know there is a "Coffee Cantata" by Bach? It seems the Emperor hated coffee houses, which were popular at that time, because he considered them centers of sedition and refused to fill HIS coffers with their bounteous revenue.

We raise our cups with thanks to Maradine's Coffee Shop. People here have many talents and interests. Let us continue to share these gifts, realizing Fellowship Square itself is a VERY SPECIAL place.

THE WALKERS AND TALKERS
By Mary Reeves

We know there is now a walking group at Fellowship Square, and we applaud them all. We want you to get to know a small group of men who have walked around this complex for over thirty-two years.

There is John Goodman. John and Adrienne have lived in Tucson for 53 years and at this place 32 years. John has been walking every morning, rain or shine, since he moved in. Along the way he has had various and numerous walkers join him. They love to end up at the Bistro just as it opens at 7 a.m. John, leader of the pack, says he wants to stay active, was never a couch potato, and loves to meet people. He has a great attitude and sense of humor, as do the two others mentioned here.

Frank and Jay Perez have lived at Fellowship Square (formerly Villas Serena) for eighteen years, moving from California. Frank began to walk with John about ten years ago. Frank says he benefits from walking, he loves meeting new people and being with friends. They not only walk but talk, and continue talking over coffee. They never run out of stories.

Speaking of stories, we now meet Red Stolle. Red is a widower, has lived here for about three years, yet everyone seems to know him and enjoy his dry wit and sense of humor. Red has a colorful past with adventures in the CIA, Navy, U.S. Customs, and more. He is an accomplished writer and computer buff, astronomer and ham radio operator. Red says he is part of the walking group for "social adjustment".

STRONG TIES
Interview by Toni Smith

Although Jeryl White and Dottie Sanford's lives were to become entwined in their later years, their beginnings were vastly different.

Jeryl was born on a ranch in Winkelman, AZ. She received all her education in Arizona, and earned her degree in Education at the University of Arizona. In 1943 Jeryl married Bryan White in Tucson. She was teaching locally when her husband, an employee at the Asarco Mining Company, was transferred to New York.

Dottie Sanford was born in St. Louis, MO., raised in Texas, and began her career as a model in New York City. She married a dashing young Air Force pilot from Bergstrom Air Force Base, who was later killed during a secret mission in the Korean War. Dottie remained a widow for three years. Then she met and married Gene, a Lieutenant at Utah General Depot. She kept busy over the next thirty years of their forty- three year marriage; moving in and out of thirty-eight different houses. Gene's work with military intelligence involved many different countries and people; his service commitments took them to many countries making those years busy, interesting and diversified. When they were living in Africa she was involved with charity works for Emperor Haile Selassie, including social engagements in and out of his palaces. These times included working, as well as charity activities and entertaining.

An interesting chapter in Jeryl's life was brought about when Bryan's work moved them to Mexico. In 1954 she became involved in teaching children in the bilingual Mexican schools after moving to Mexico, and later in 1968 in Mexico City. She has wonderful stories about her times with the children in Mexico. In 1973 they returned to New York where Bryan became VP of Southern Peru Copper Corp. They often traveled to Peru until retirement.

For both couples, 1980 was retirement year, although Gene was still on active recall. Within three months of each other they moved to Corona De Tucson. Unknowingly they were within six blocks of each other, near a golf course. They had never met, but when they did there was an indefinable attraction which drew them together as a close family of four. The husbands became acquainted first, with Jeryl and Dottie following shortly thereafter. There was time for volunteer work which had always been a part of both women's lives, and the men found a project they could delve into full force: a fire department for Corona De Tucson. It was badly needed for the fast growing area, and they were just the ones who could accomplish the deed. The two men's background gave them a great deal of expertise; Gene's military intelligence, and Bryan a leading expert in Management. The project was their inspiration—starting with the plans, getting the builder, right through to the opening day. It took three years. Bryan became president, Gene vice president, and later Jeryl was secretary of the board. One of the long lasting effects of their endeavor, which made both Gene and Bryan very proud, was the fact that the residents of the area had their insurance bill cut in half.

Later, Bryan developed cancer which brought the men closer. After Bryan died, Jeryl, Dottie and Gene became the three musketeers. Gene remained as an R.A. full Colonel until he died, from complications concurred while serving in the Vietnam War. When Dottie developed health problems of a serious nature, Jeryl saw she was well taken care of.

Today they live here as close friends with deep respect and admiration for each other. It is heartwarming to know them and hear their story. Reading between the lines, one knows there is much more to this story than appears here. Commitment, need, compassion, love and respect are only a few of the strong ties of this ageless and enduring friendship.

THE APPEAL OF APPLAUSE
Interview by Toni Smith

Joe and Joyce Grass, fellow residents, came to Arizona after Joe's retirement, from Brookfield, Wisconsin. After their daughter moved to Tucson they paid her a visit, and the couple fell in love with the Tucson area, however they later choose to settle in Green Valley.

Joyce and Joe had met in the 9th grade and their friendship blossomed into a lifelong relationship. Joe graduated from the Milwaukee School of Engineering. He was a movie projectionist, while attending college which helped pay his tuition and enhance his resume in years to come.

Joe was eligible for military service upon graduation from college, and spent five years in the Army, 1940-45, which included three years in the Pacific. The couple decided they would not marry until after the war, and Joyce worked as a secretary during Joe's absence. After recovering from a service connected illness, Joe started his career with G.E. Medical systems in the field of medical diagnostic imaging, connected with heart research. He acquired six patents during his career, five from the United States, and one from Europe. Joe retired after working 28 years for G.E. Joe and Joyce traveled for some time, and then settled into a new home in Green Valley.

Retirement did not mean sitting around and doing nothing to Joe and Joyce. They were active and energetic so became involved in volunteer work. It was after they joined the Green Valley Elks that a new career began for them. Performing! Perfect, and they were ready. Church variety shows and Joe's jobs during his college years helped prepare them for this venture. If you have ever participated in performing, then you know how exciting it can be, and how much work and time goes into each endeavor. Joe was a natural. No amount of rehearsal time was too much, and any technical problem was immediately tackled with energizing fervor. Joyce joined him in these productions making costumes and participating in the performances. At one time she had done Phyllis Diller impersonations—they were a pair!

Two of his more popular skits were a roast of one of the members of the Elk's, based on Red Buttons performance, and his other was The Great Flydini, the magician, taken from a Steve Martin's repertoire. Flydini took eight months to perfect with Joyce making the costume and acting as his side kick on stage. The skit required tireless effort in working out all the mechanics and technicalities.

Talking to Joe one can feel the anticipation and excitement he felt before each production. Waiting for the curtain to open! The first glimpse of the audience waiting, anticipating his performance. Show time! The people loved the performances and the laughter was spontaneous, and boisterous. There were many curtain calls with loud and prolonged applause. Joyce and Joe were on a roll and they loved it.

Joe was honored as Elk of the year in 1994. He called Bingo and performed many other duties in between variety shows, during the seventeen years he and Joyce participated in the Elks. The audience reaction and applause touched his heart, but the real appeal of performing was what he gave to the audience. He's a natural!

THE GOOD LIFE
By Toni Smith

In 1971, Villas Serenas was built as a luxury, resort-style apartment complex, encompassing ten-acres, and made up of four separate "Villas", each with a separate manager. Villa Serenas soon boasted five swimming pools, four of which were heated, along with tennis courts and golf facilities which featured well-manicured putting greens and putting range. When completed, Villa Serenas sat atop the hill on Broadway Boulevard and was surrounded by beautiful desert views and featured lush landscaping. Thirty-five years ago, John and Adrienne Goodman moved into an apartment in the newly completed Villa Four, in Villa Serenas. This was to be only a temporary move, as they had in mind building a home of their own to replace the house they had recently sold in Tucson. John and Adrienne had come from Canada and become American citizens, and had lived in Southern Arizona for over twenty years. Settling into their "brand new" apartment, they soon found apartment living very comfortable, and found many activities to keep them busy and entertained.

Adrienne tells of how Villas Serenas attracted many popular personalities from many different areas. There were golf enthusiasts who came to Tucson for the different tournaments and made Villas Serenas their home base during their stay. Movie stars also came; film star Forrest Tucker, rented an apartment while filming and was often seen enjoying the parties and gatherings, especially those in Villa 4. TV star Liz Carter was also known to rent an apartment at Villas Serenas, and often participated in the many social activities offered to residents. Snowbirds and Winter Visitors also found the Villas an attractive escape during the winter months.

Tucson's rodeos and parade were a big attraction then, as they are now. John was semi-retired, but still active in real estate. He and Adrienne would keep busy with local activities and Adrienne often rode in the Rodeo parade on one of the decorated flatbed trailers, pulled by horses. John and Adrienne were active square dancers and loved to take part in the many parties that were offered in Villa 4. They would often contribute to the social gatherings by helping with the decorations for a pool party or by providing hors d'oeuvres during one of the many "cocktail hours."

In the days of Villas Serenas, there was not a Dining Room on the premises, but that was not a problem; there were many excellent "eateries" in the area. Furr's Cafeteria was very popular at that time and was conveniently located where Park Place Mall later came into being. John and Adrienne watched the eastside grow around them over the years—with businesses coming and going and further expansion and growth.

In 2001, Christian Care Companies purchased Villa Serenas and made it into a resort-style, Senior retirement community for adults, 62 and older, encompassing all four separate Villas into one entity with Activities available for the whole community; Villa Serenas became Fellowship Square Tucson. In 2002 the Dining Room was completed providing not only a convenient dining location for the residents, but also a location for special community meetings and entertainment. Shortly after opening the Dining Room, a library and computer lab were made available. Fellowship Square Tucson became an extremely active place. People hustle and bustle from Villa to Villa to engage in the programs offered daily and during the weekends, along with the many activities carried on in each "Villa" Clubhouse. People meet in the dining room to enjoy a delicious meal and visit with friends and neighbors, or enjoy breakfast or lunch in the Bistro Cafe; and we all eagerly await the daily mail delivery in the individual Villa's mail rooms; socializing and catching up.

There is no Utopia, we all know that. However, this might be as close as it gets considering how much we have provided for us in this community. We, as "mature" individuals have the right to disagree and complain—free speech is guaranteed—but for most of us, we are thankful we are here. We as residents were asked on a recent survey: "Where would you live if you did not live here?" The answer probably would be for most of us, our own homes; we have however, "matured" past that point now, so this is just FINE, and we are happy here.

THE PIPER OF FELLOWSHIP SQUARE
Interview by Toni Smith

A lust for life and a joy for living describe Jim Stirling, a resident of Fellowship Square since 1994. While Jim's wife was living, they both enjoyed the many activities and opportunities here. At 98, Jim still maintains a full calendar of social activities, physical fitness, swimming and Tai-chi.

Jim was born in Dundee, Scotland. His love of Scotland has been passed along to his children and their families. He is proud of his ancestry and took his family on trips to his homeland, so they all have fond memories of Scotland. When Jim was twelve years old he joined the "Boys Brigade", playing the bagpipes and grew to love the music of the pipes. He left school at fourteen and went to work. Many of the boys were forced to stop their schooling because their families were poor, and it was necessary for them to work to survive.

In 1923, when he was nineteen, his father brought him to the United States, entering the U.S. through Ellis Island. His father got a job and worked hard to get all his family to this country. Later, after the family was together, they moved to Hoosick, New York. Jim went to night school to finish his education. His father became a tool maker and they moved to Pittsfield, Massachusetts where Jim also became a tool maker and worked for General Electric for twenty-eight years.

Jim kept up with his Bag Pipe playing. He found another hobby, which he, his wife and their family thoroughly enjoyed; hiking. Jim has hiked many a trail and climbed many a mountain in many states. Maine; Mt Washington New Hampshire; the Teton Mountains in Jackson Hole, Wyoming and the Appalachian Trail. Bear Canyon, Rincon Mountains and Sabino Canyon, Arizona, to mention just a few.

When Jim retired, they moved to Bellevue, Nebraska. Jim and his wife began a whirlwind of activities in the field of volunteering. They worked with handicapped children of all ages at the Chapp School. Jim and his wife were prominent in working at the senior center, leading singing activities, dances and other social events. They were a popular couple wherever they went. Jim has received many awards and plaques of recognition honoring his Bag Pipe playing. One such plaque was received from the Tucson Celtic Festival in 1977, for 70 years of Outstanding Music Contribution. Jim's family is the focus point in his life. One of his fondest memories is that he "Bag Piped" his daughters into their wedding ceremonies.

His daughter Sandi, who lives in Pinetop with her family, spends quality time with Jim, and has put together marvelous photo albums covering a colorful and interesting history of her parent's lives. Jim has played "Amazing Grace" many times in his life. When Jim smiles, you can see a man of amazing grace.

Charles Stone—Daisies

CHAPTER THREE

On Leaving The Nest

Oh those were the days! Or were they? Are those memories of "Days gone by" colored by time and our desire to re-write them to our liking?

Growing up can be pleasantly rewarding or awkwardly embarrassing...often at the same time.

ANTHONY
By Stella Klepac

Anthony must have looked like this,
(Though I have loving prejudice)
When he was a little boy;
(And that was only yesterday)
With chuckles and shouted joy,
Going his merry, lurching way—
Colliding with passersby,
His two tiny fists a-fly;
On dimpled sturdy legs and strong,
Small feet castanet-ing along.
Like this he must have been,
Like this little laughing lark;
Tousled curls of black sheen,
Eyes of brown and lashed so dark.
Thus was my Tony when he was small –
My Tony who's now grown so tall!

BERMUDA By Red Stolle

Due to the limitations imposed on the writer by the F.S.A.O., this story will be short. The readers are urged to use their imagination to fill in the blanks, because most of the good stuff will be left out. The main character will be referred to as Mr. He.

Mister He was tired of his lifestyle working at the Pentagon, and decided to change it. He went to the University and took many aptitude tests and was told to become a Naval Officer, Writer, or a Charter Boat Skipper. He decided to become a Charter Boat Skipper, got a sailboat, and sailed out into the dangerous Atlantic Ocean to the small island of Bermuda.

After two days, in the Gulf Stream, he spotted a giant dorsal fin more than eight feet tall coming straight at him. He thought it was a sea monster. He got scared and went down in his cabin to hide. He expected a resounding crash, but no crash or crunch came. He stayed below for several hours reading all he could about big fishes and sea monsters. He came out on deck and all was quiet. Later that night, something happened.

He could not believe what he saw—his cabin was full of light almost like daylight. Out on deck he saw thousands of Dolphins all dancing around his little boat. Everything was so bright; he could read a book or a newspaper.

Another two days of wonderful sailing, then a giant storm hit his boat. The storm lasted for two days or more. He had tied himself to the mizzenmast to keep from being washed overboard. Down below he was thrown from one end to another. Afraid of breaking his ribs, he forced himself into the quarter berth and fell asleep. Upon waking he found his small boat was sinking. He found the leak, fixed it, and pumped his boat out within a few minutes of sinking; then he sailed to Bermuda.

Upon reaching Bermuda, the Royal Bermuda Yacht Club repaired his boat. He made many new friends. The TV Station put him on Television to tell his story; He told everyone he was on an extended coffee break from the Pentagon, and decided to sail to Bermuda.

BOUNCING BETTY'S
By Red Stolle

From my tent located at a newly constructed base on the Admiralty Islands just north of New Guinea, I could see across the bay several ships at anchor. They seemed to be waiting for hungry guys like myself to visit them for some cold water and maybe ice cream. As young Navy Ensign, navigating a large patrol plane was easy compared to walking through the jungle alone. Nevertheless, the White Sands of the beach with its many tall coconut palm trees was an alluring invitation to go exploring again.

With my machete and pistol in hand, I started walking down towards the beach. Following the water's edge, I looked for an inroad or a trail to lead me to the jungle. There, not far away, was an opening into the jungle. The opening merged into a trail that showed signs of travel, but was covered with green vegetation. I had to use my machete to clear my way along the trail. It seemed very dark; the heavy vegetation was blocking the sunlight, leaving a dark and mysterious trail.

As I followed the trail, it appeared that I was coming to a clearing with some kind of activity. I expected to see the Australian coast watcher and the wild cannibals again. But no, this time looking around a bend in the trail I was looking straight at several hundred Japanese; they all seem to be looking right at me. No gunshots or loud voices, all was quiet. I looked again and saw the Japanese soldiers lying on the ground. The sweet smell of Saki was everywhere. They must have had one heck of a party, and they were now all dead. At least I hoped so. I said to myself, "Don't anyone move."

My trail was covered with dead Japanese soldiers. I was going to have to walk over all of them to get to the other side to continue following the trail. They had not been there very long, and looked very lifelike, which scared me. Pistol in hand I began to pick my way over the top of these dead soldiers, each step was followed by a deep complaining groan, to my ears they sounded very much alive. It was all very unsettling, and I wanted to get away as soon as possible.

Something was moving—I saw from the corner of my eye some brown uniforms moving around - from one Japanese soldier to another. I soon realized they were U.S. Army personnel doing something I just couldn't believe: Each one had a pair of pliers, and was extracting the gold teeth from the dead Japanese soldiers. It was not a happy sight. They were so busy pulling teeth that I passed unnoticed.

As I walked on I began to notice there were less and less trees. I could see some movement again, I looked and there were some more soldiers at a distance doing something, but what were they doing?

It looked like they were waving at me and shouting. I could not tell what they were trying to say. Maybe they were glad to see me. I couldn't understand them. I moved closer and closer. The closer I got, the more exaggerated their shouts, and actions, but I still didn't understand them. I later found out they were Australian bomb disposal personnel. They were calling me all kinds of bloody names, warning me to stop, but I didn't until I reached them. They told me I just walked through a Japanese Minefield without exploding any of the "Bouncing Betty's". I was a very lucky man that day. Someone must have been watching over me.

CHIVALRY IS DEAD
By Jeanne Nylander

He smiled, held the car door open wide
So his trim little wife could step inside.
The reason—certainly one of two,
Either the wife or the car is new!!

HOUSE FOR SALE
By Elsie Hobbs

One day a sign appeared at my curb. It said HOUSE FOR SALE. It was just a statement. A house was for sale. But it meant a lot more than that to me. I was for sale and I was very sad. I should not have been surprised that you decided to sell your home. I should have suspected it. I also felt the loss. I knew it was getting to be more and more difficult for you to live here, in his home, without him. After all, I was his home before you came into his life and before that, I had been his parent's home.

Love makes a house a home. I was filled with happiness when I was a home for the two of you. His children came to visit. Your children came to visit. The grandchildren came and after a time they brought great grandchildren. Love filled every one of my rooms. The love that the two of you had for each other overflowed into the yard and on to the back lot. The back lot was his special place. It was vacant and he kept it raked so clean. Neighbors commented about it always being so neat. To him it was the ultimate. He was never happier than when he stood in the middle of that vacant lot to just look around. He really enjoyed his space.

Then one day the two of you went on a trip. You came back without him. It was never the same after that. No, I should not have been surprised that you decided to sell me. You will be pleased to know that I like my new owner and I think she likes me. I know I am a very special place. I overheard her talking to some friends. She told them that she could actually feel the love that the two of you shared here. I would have been just a house without your love. It was your love that made me a home. When you could no longer live here without him, that sign at the curb should have said HOME FOR SALE.

GETAWAYS
By Mary Reeves

How do I love thee
Let me count the ways
Woe is me I must be
Back in only three more days!!

I'm off to a style show
I'm all dressed up
I have wanted to do this
Since Heck was a pup

You said you'd go fishing
I packed all your gear
Now do me a favor an
Get out of here!!

IF I COULD SING
By Stella Klepac

Love, if I could sing,
I'd sing to cheer your heart;
I'd sing of life and spring,
And how I'm ever longing,
When we must be apart.

Each day I'd wake you with a tune,
And chant of love beneath the moon;
I'd hold you close within my arms,
And croon a tender lullaby,
I'd tell you of your manly charms—
Your strength, your smile, your sparkling eye—
In praise of you my voice would ring,
Love, if I could only sing!

LEARNING ABOUT ANTIQUES
By Toni Smith

My first learning experience re: antiquing, surfaced when I was browsing through "Antique" and "Old Attic" store on the Seattle water front with my daughters. Gazing at a shelf above where we were standing I saw a wicker doll carriage just like the one I had as a little girl. I dearly loved that carriage, and was about to say so to the girls, when one of them spoke out in a loud voice,

"Yuck, look at that ugly old doll carriage. Gross!" They quickly moved on. I followed them making no comment.

As we moved on through the store, I looked for a hand egg-beater. There were times when I could use one, and I had been looking lately without success. I found one. "Just what I've been looking for." I said sort of to myself.

Sure enough, a voice whispered in my ear, "Why do you want that old thing? You have a Cuisenaire with all the attachments." My daughter turned and headed toward the door with the other girls and I followed without comment.

Later in a tiny grocery store I was going to ask if they sold Lard, for making pie crust, but I thought twice about it and walked out of the store, relieved that the girls had not followed me.

Our next stop was an old department store with various items scattered around in no particular order. I had something in mind and told the girls they could browse on their own. I was feeling pouty and grumpy about their attitude. They moved on…A clerk came by carrying a load of old pans she was moving to a different area. I stopped her and asked, "Do you happen to have one of those ten or twelve inch black spiders?"—the clerk quickly moved away, "Iron skillets," I muttered. After a moment of stunned silence she said, "Ma'am I don't think so, but I will ask my supervisor."

Before I could stop her she went scurrying away dropping one of the pans which went clattering on to the wooden floor and under the counter. I shuddered. The noise attracted the girls' attention and they came back to see what was going on. I was going to walk away in the opposite direction but was detained when the clerk dragging the supervisor behind her appeared directly in front of me. "You were inquiring about a black spider…ten or twelve inches?" the supervisor asked me. The girls looked at me in horror.

One of the girls spoke to me in a disgusted voice, "We're not in a Zoo, Mom. Really!"

"Yes, I was thinking about it, but have changed my mind." I answered the supervisor.

"Please, Ma'am, we could talk to the Manager if you wish." I could feel hands grabbing my coat sleeves.

"No, that's all right." I felt my self being propelled toward the door. As we stepped outside the girls spotted a coffee shop. I told them to go ahead and would be there shortly. Another challenge. "Coffee shops" with all those fancy names were an enigma to me. I waited until they were happily chatting away sipping, Espresso coffee. I walked down to join them and studied the Espresso menu on the Starbucks Coffee blackboard, which was like reading Greek to me. I decided what to order, went up to the counter and in a firm voice ordered, "One mocha, heavy on the cream, frappucino!"

Waiting for my order to be filled, I turned to look at the girls. Broad smiles wreathed their faces and they motioned me to sit down.

"Where to now, Mom?" one of the girls asked. "I'm content just to sit here awhile and enjoy my frappe. Why don't you go browsing, and I'll meet you by the car in an hour."

All agreed. The girls went down the street chattering to each other as I sat, surveyed the scenery and sipped my drink. Suddenly I realized that I was not alone. My "invisible" friend, whom I discovered in my bathroom mirror, who looks like me, (but older of course) and follows me everywhere was beside me smiling. "Learn anything?" she smirked.

"Yes, it is better to shop with well preserved antiques than for antiques."

"Takes one to know one," whispered my friend.

LITTLE SOLDIER
By Stella Klepac

So you were born and you're stuck with it,
Not having any luck with it,
And the battle still goes on.

Some you have lost and some you have won,
But all of your life you have carried your gun,
You haven't turned tail and run.

Lay down that gun and take a little rest;
Shrug your shoulders and make a little jest.
Then march again into the fray,
Another chance, another day.

Suck in your gut, little soldier,
Suck in your gut.

Hold up your head and stick out your chin—
Some you will lose and some you will win.

George Erickson—Roman Soldier

LOVE HAPPENS
By Elsa Stinger

Joanne and Bob met at a party

At his house, no less.

Lots to eat, a place to swim,

Bob's many friends fit right in.

Music, sunshine, kids galore

And much more

Both looking for love

And it was right there at Bob's door.

To a proposal,

In a couple of years,

Love to devotion.

Much to discuss-families met,

Both older, educated, and employed.

Plans to make, future agreed upon

Just one catch or two to discuss yet.

Joanne said to Bob, "Accept my two cats."

Bob said to Joanne...

                              "If no golf, wedding's off!"

MOOCHIE SQUIRREL AND THE THANKSGIVING NUT
By Gene Guerreno

Moochie Squirrel found a fine, fat Nut under a big tree.
Moochie was hungry." Here is my dinner!" he thought.
Moochie turned the nut UP… he turned the nut DOWN…
Moochie looked at the nut – Close Up and way Down,
Far away!

How do you open a Nut? Moochie looked some more.
He dropped it – HARD! – Nothing…
Moochie squee-ee-zed that Nut. Nope.
Moochie sat on the Nut… No way!

Think! Grandpa opened nuts – Grandma could, too
Uncles… Aunts…Cousins… HMMMM.
Moochie put that big, fat, fine nut in his mouth …
To keep it safe while he thought… AND!

Before Moochie could get his paw out of his mouth,
He closed it …. Hard! OW! Crunch! AH HAH!
THAT'S The way a squirrel would eat a big Fat Nut
For his Thanksgiving Dinner!

Aren't you glad Yours are already opened?

STILL...TWO

By Gene Guerreno

You

Can Not

Cry my Tears

Chortle my Laugh

Ache Deep with my Pain

For "I" am "I"—"You"—"You"…

If this be true… tell me "Why"

Your tears burn my eyes when you –cry-?

Your pain … tears my Soul with Agony?

If this be Love—Pray call me Enemy!

Charles Stone—The Catch

THE DAY WE BECAME AMERICANS
By Frances McCreadie

My husband and I, born in Canada, had spent half a life time there. Now he was offered a transfer to the United States as a manager in his field of expertise; building materials of brick, tile and stone. This momentous decision made, we settled happily into our new lifestyle. Our decision was to become American citizens after the five-year waiting period.

What would we need to know? We were told an oral examination would only ask for what any American citizen should know. But what does an average American know? That was my project for the next time-frame. I spent noon-hour breaks studying American History and Geography until I felt I could locate every state, its capitol, and describe its exports and climates with some degree of accuracy. I also taught myself some facts about the government and how it operates. This involved two or three visits to the consulate in Buffalo, New York.

Finally came the important day we would be questioned. What questions? We would lose our Canadian citizenship and become Americans. For moral support I invited a friend to go with us, but would that be any help? All I had studied seemed to fade away, and I felt like a child being called to the front of the class when my name was called. My questioner looked properly serious as we faced one another. I knew my husband too, was being questioned in some other room but he would impress them with his confident attitude and brilliant answers. What would I be asked?

My questioner looked at me and simply said. "Who is the Vice-President?" As he waited for an answer I simply could not recall. I, who had studied the line of succession of the kings and queens on the British thrones, could discuss the Magna Carta or the Battle of Hastings, stood mute. I thought he sighed. With a glance at the ceiling and in a tone half-disgusted and half-resigned he said it for me. Spiro Agnew was the answer spoken in a voice that did me no favors. A wave of his hand indicated the interview was over and I had passed the test. The bar had been lowered for me and I had surmounted it.

The rest of the ceremony was more relaxed. We listened to welcoming speeches and shook many important hands. We repeated the pledge of allegiance and received the important papers of citizenship. Returning home, we felt we had done something important and memorable.

I had resolved never to tell my husband how poorly I had tested but the secret was too big to contain and it soon became a part of our family history.

THOSE WERE THE DAYS
By Jeanne Nylander

My friend was a very dejected old soul.

A dejected old soul was he,

We were talking about the "good old days"

And he could only remember three!!!

Dottie Kath—Horse In A Field

THE HOUSE
By George Gardiner

Good-bye House!
>   I'm sorry that I must leave you
>   But you've grown old
>   And must be sold
>   Now please don't let me grieve you.

I'll long remember
>   The day when first I met you
>   You then were new
>   And life was too
>   'Tis sure I'll never forget you.

Remember when
>   We had our first big party?
>   The fun and laughter
>   And silence after
>   When we toasted you so hearty.

Remembering
>   The sound of rain and windy trees
>   Through the years
>   Of smiles and tears
>   On love's Book of Golden Leaves.

The Special Times,
>   That left our hearts a gleaming
>   The candlelight's
>   On Christmas nights
>   And lovely hours just dreaming.

So, good-bye, house
>   For those that here will dwell
>   We know that you
>   Will love them too
>   And so we say, farewell.

Hello House!

> I'm pleased with your creation
> When you were made
> Each brick was laid
> With loving adoration.

I'll long remember,

> The joys you gave a-borning
> On a silent knoll
> I stirred your soul
> One early dew-kissed morning.

I scarce can wait

> Until your rooms are lighted
> I've dreams to make
> And naps to take
> And a thousand hopes required.

In days ahead

> Through sun and rolling storm
> Our lives will blend
> Until they end
> With love that's new and warm

So, Hello House!

> I'm proud as I can be
> I'll keep you fair
> With loving care
> If you'll be a home for me!

THE NEW WEST
By George Gardiner

The ways of the "Old West" are rapidly fading into oblivion; there is little question about that. What about the "New West"? Are the thousands moving to Arizona just looking for a better climate, or relief for their arthritis? I think many of our Old Timers are adopting the lifestyle and dress of incoming Easterners. What a pity! Recently I saw a man in a Sonoita restaurant, whom I know has lived here for years, wearing shorts and floppies! I could have retched! I believe the highly regarded spirit and code of the Arizonans before us would benefit us all today if we would practice it. I, for one, Mr. Newcomer, would hope that when you cross the Arizona border you would become a westerner, not an easterner living in the west. Buy some western clothes, a pair of boots, a bolo, a wide brimmed hat, a belt and buckle. If you are going to live in the West, dress like it! You'll soon learn why these are items of choice by the natives.

Next, learn how to pronounce javalina, ocotillo, Tumacacori, saguaro, a few other western words. Learn about horses and buy one if you can. You'll have to learn a few more things… from which side do you mount. What and how much do you feed a horse.

Be sure to buy a book or books that will tell you the history and location of Arizona's numerous ghost towns, old mines, and points of historic. If you are interested in becoming a "Westerner", I recommend a trip to the town of Wilcox, home of the Rex Allenn Museum, Bisbee and the old Copper Queen hotel, Tombstone steeped in the wild days of the early West. Be sure to make a trip to Nogales, cross the border and walk the length of the street known as Obregon. Silver, leather, onyx, carvings, and more…and while you're there, buy something! It's the neighborly thing to do.

By now you should begin to fell a little like John Wayne, you can refer to a Mohave Green with confidence, and will have learned to never ask a rancher the number of cattle he has (that's like asking how much money he has). You no longer need to wonder who Cochise, Geronimo, or Victorio was. You can tell your relatives back in New Jersey about talking to a working waddle who told you how he punched a hole in his rope and brought down a wild steer. By now you're getting pretty close to being a man of the West. Now you know the wisdom of leather boots in snake country, and the shade furnished by a wide-brimmed hat. You can say Buenos Diaz, Hasta la Vista, Muy Bien, and Gracias with ease. Now you can chuckle when a new comer tries to pronounce "Octoillo". Now you can eat your steaks rare, gobble down jalapenos like peanuts, and drink Margaritas till the coyotes fall asleep.

However, my newcomer friend from Steeltown, PA, I think it's only fair to tell you that even though it's a wonderful idea, there are a few facts that are often overlooked when one buys a horse. First, the horse has to have a place to live. Your fenced backyard won't do. No... Sparkplug will need a stable and corral (with water piped in). Then, if you intend to ride you will need a saddle, a bridle and halter, a saddle blanket, a curry comb and brush, a hoof pick, shoes every few weeks, and hay and pellets every day.

Discouraging? Don't let it be. A good saddle horse is a great companion. I have always said, "The world looks different from the back of a horse." Oh... one thing more, your wife is almost sure to want a horse of her own. Just bite the leather and buy her one.

"O.K. Partner, I'll meet you by the corral, we'll ride out, punch a hole in our ropes and go lasso a Toro!"

TIME HAS NOT BEEN KIND
By Suzanne Harvor

Do not stand there gazing at me with anxious eyes
Looking for traces of the sparkling girl you knew
Now perhaps hiding behind the hooded eyes and sagging jowls.
Unrecognizable.

If you could see my mind you might remember me
At least a trace of who I am or was.
But even that is crumbling around the edges.
I sense the weighty dough surround and seep inwards.
Some day the lump you see will be all there is.

Flying thoughts race past fumbling fingers.
Left behind the sleek silver sheen of wit.
Needed words lie hidden in the mist
Or crowd, jumbled, on the page.
The delicate graceful mind is not lurking
Safely behind the crumbling façade
Of my face.

My mind likes to sit quietly now
In a dark green forest not remembered
Or perhaps never known.
The peace of nowhere nothingness.
This is what death should be like.

YEARLY AND DEARLY
By Stella Klepac

Ya gotta have a birthday, Dear,
Ya gotta have one every year;

Ya gotta have a ton of fun
And count your blessings one by one—
And also count the candles!

Ya gotta show up for your party;
Ya gotta be there hale and hearty.

Ice cream, cake and Whoop-di-doo
And may all your dreams come true—
Or, at least some of them!

Presents, pals and reminiscing;
Hugs and squeezes and lots of kissing.

May your birthday bring you joys galore;
And may you have a hundred more!

CHAPTER FOUR

A Flight Of Fancy

Sometimes you get ideas that are not worth flapping your wings about, not inspiring or necessarily challenging. Just important thoughts that are worth sharing.

Just relax and enjoy the following pages as we let the prevailing currents carry us along to nowhere in particular.

A DREAM TO DREAM
By Ruth Spitzer

When I was six or seven or eight
Ginger Rogers I would emulate
Fred Astair would lift me high
And fling me up in the sky

My chiffon gown filled the air
And we moved with a graceful flair
To twirl and soar as the music played
These were the happiest of my days

I practiced every day assiduously
But to be a klutz is my destiny
I have the option to watch a movie or TV
And it's not Ginger, you see, it's really me

AN ORGAN RECITAL
By Elsie Hobbs

Let me tell you about my operation, wait! Don't turn off those hearing aids. If you do, you are going to miss a very different Organ Recital.

It was a very, very, long time ago. I was still in my teens. I had a major surgery. They cut my abdominal area from the top to the bottom. It was from as far up as possible to as far down as possible. I am not going to go into the details of all the rearranging that went on during the operation. That isn't what this is all about. It is all about <u>what I lost.</u> It's what I lost during that operation that has had a lasting effect on me. Have you any idea what that could have been?

I lost my belly button. That's right. I don't have a belly button. I know. Once you are born you never need a belly button again. That is what I was told. You'll never need it again. But I missed it.

It was a great place to keep the salt when I ate celery in bed. Without it I had no hope to ever become a famous Belly Dancer. Who ever heard of a Belly Dancer without a belly button. There were times I was actually embarrassed because I had no belly button.

I will never forget my physical exam when I enlisted in the Women's Army during WW II. There I was stripped down. You know the routine. The doctor said to the nurse, "how do you suppose she got born?" She never batted an eye as she responded, "Damned if I know. She must have been an incubator baby".

ANOTHER CHRISTMAS
By Mary Reeves

It's Christmas again! I can hardly wait
I'm older this year so I may be late

Turkey and dressing, potatoes galore
Cakes and pies – give me more!!

(This all sounds familiar – have we done it before?)

My memory is failing so others tell me
"your don't need your car – are you sure you can see?"
"we'll watch your money – you're almost broke"

Wait a minute just hold it – Is this a joke?

Aren't children wonderful? They know it all.
Hand me my checkbook – I'm off to the mall.

CHAIR DANCING
By Ellen Canterbury

We are the past ballerinas.

We danced a different tune,

We spun, we twirled,

We danced, we whirled.

Now in our chairs we dream

Of where we've been.

We move cautiously,

But we move,

Our arms, our legs.

We stand, we sit.

We are in a different world

But still remember where we've been.

GOD
(He may have feelings, too!)
By Charlie Stone

Did God get it started,

Say "That's good!" and then parted

Just to count his sparrows all day?

Did He give us a voice

In making a choice

Without insisting we do it His way?

I just may be slightly

Anthropomorphic, it's likely.

But, there's reason to believe, I'm afraid,

That God is incontinent

And seems to be content

Simply to rain on my parade!

But, could it be that He's sad about

The way that I've turned out,

And I should take back the things I've said?

Could it be He was trying,

And just wound up crying

And those drops were His tears instead?

HAIKU
By Ellen Canterbury

Wind, water, eons
Formed over centuries…
It's a Grand Canyon

Ugly javelina,
No graceful touch was given
To this awkward beast!

Wind creates patterns
In waves and white caps at sea
In golden wheat fields

Flashing bright colors,
Butterflies skim flower tops…
What a joyful sight!

JEFFERSON
By Laura McCoy

Someone should have told Jefferson that if you look like a duck, and walk like a duck, you must be a duck. Unfortunately that didn't happen.

Jefferson arrived one Easter morning on the doorstep with a note attached that read, "You like strange pets, how about this one?"

They must have been referring to the squirrel that adopted us in the winter and liked his grapes peeled and to drink from a glass of Pepsi, maybe it was the little brown mouse with the cute pink ears who lived in our big plant in the family room, or it could have been the cat that conned his way in one rainy morning after Jack had said, "No, you can't bring that bedraggled stray into the house."

That "stray" stayed twenty two more years.

Jefferson was the cutest little ball of fluff. He came prepaid with a bag of mash and a clean box. He definitely was a duck.

As Jefferson (I don't know who named him) grew to be a teen-ager, he became the ugliest creature around. His fluff fell out and his pin feathers grew in as scraggly as a month old beard.

In no time at all he decided who his "mother" was. It was the one who got up at night to wind the clock for his box when he couldn't sleep. It was the one who had to see that his water dish hadn't turned over from those big, flat feet. It was the one who fed him three times a day and let him run around the room and clean up after him.

Jefferson soon outgrew and out-pooped every box we could find to keep him in. Finally, we had to put him out on the patio with only a chicken wire fence to keep him safe. One day as I hung up the laundry and let him out to catch the bugs in the yard, he thought it was a game to grab the clothes as I shook them out to hang on the line. He soon learned to play "Tug of war". He could really hang on tight.

Although Jefferson was a "house duck" he nevertheless soon began to associate with the older teenagers in the house. He rode on the handlebars of Bob's bike with the aid of an old shirt he could grip. Then he graduated to the gas tank of Phil's motorcycle. That was something to see – a big white duck riding on a motorcycle.

Jeff made friends with the school kids as they walked by the house every morning. Sometimes they would stop and talk to him. I didn't worry about it until one morning a little boy knocked on the door with Jeff in his arms, and said the duck had followed him all the way to the corner. He was no longer allowed in the yard until school started. If any stray dogs attempted to come into the yard they were met with angry hisses and loud quack until the retreated. He didn't like dogs.

Unfortunately Jeff developed a bad habit. We could no longer enjoy our evening cocktail in the yard unless we kept a firm grip on the glass. You see, someone had left his glass on the ground near his chair, and we found Jeff staggering around unable to keep his balance on those over-sized feet. My, how Jeff enjoyed those evening "happy hours".

Summer grew into autumn and Jefferson began sitting under the Spirea bushes. One morning as I called he seemed reluctant to leave his haven. I went over to see if he was okay and discovered two large eggs in his hiding place. Oh, my gosh, here we had called her Jefferson all this time, when it should have been Josephine. From then on we enjoyed duck eggs, they are really good to eat.

Josephine had to leave us as winter became to cold for her to live outside, so we took her to a farmer who lived just outside the city limits. She still came when we called to her, but you could see she enjoyed the comfort of living in the hen house with more of her feathered friends.

I NEED TIME!!!
By Mary Reeves

It is at the least disappointing to realize I will be 79 my next birthday! If I could get away with it I would cut 5 years off my life. I recently had an aunt die who perpetually lied about her age - - always making her age just 2 years older then I am, despite the fact that she was 8 years older!! But no, there was no truth even in death – her tombstone says the year she had chosen to be born, not the real one, but more power to her!

Look at the things I still need time to do:

- Read everything in my house worth reading—that would take at least a year!!

- Study the life of Paul!! How exciting.

- Practice Yoga—meditate

- Grow sprouts in my kitchen.

- Write a book, or short story

- Crochet

- Think about my life – am I a real person?—What can I do to make myself and others happy?

- Straighten out my closets and drawers!

Time is passing so fast, and today is important – every day is!

MAMA KITTY
By Lorraine Smith

Mama Kitty was born about nine years ago in the alley under an abandoned car. With the help of animal experts we managed to capture all the babies and all were adopted, with the exception of Mama Kitty. She was not to be found!

On her own Mama Kitty came back, and lived on my patio, in a bed under a table.

I had adopted "pokey", an orange and white house cat. He would venture onto the patio and amazingly he and mama kitty became friends. Mama never lived in a house, nor had anyone ever touched her – with the exception of animal experts.

After 30 years in my home and in my eighties, I knew I needed to downsize. I found my new home at fellowship square. Again the animal experts came to my rescue. Sensing a change Mama had again vanished. The people who bought my house allowed me to leave a trap in the driveway, hoping mama cat would come back.

Two weeks after I had moved I got a call that Mama Cat had returned and was in the trap. I asked animal experts to take her to the vet and get needed exam and shots. When she was ready to leave, the vet's animal experts brought her to me and said "good luck". They were not so sure this was a good thing.

Pokey was on the bed asleep, and when I opened the cage door, not knowing what was to happen, Mama leaped up on the bed and began to knead pokey. My joy was complete when my two cats kissed! Mama is truly "at home".

MY FIRST DATE IN FIFTY YEARS!
By Mary Reeves

I finally had a real date!! After 47 years of marriage and three years widowed I have yet to find anyone interesting.

My friend, Lorraine, mentioned she had a friend 7 years younger than me, a widower, and he wrote poems. What else could I ask?

The next day Lorraine and I met Tom in the parking lot. He had "dressed up" for the occasion – I had on a flouncy short skirt and dangling earrings.

He looked far older then I did (I thought). He also seemed to have trouble with his feet, so slow getting to the dining room. I got ahead of him and he yelled "I have bunions" – "Good to know" I answered.

Throughout lunch, (and he ate every bite), he read some of his poems, which I found long and tedious. He would then say: "Your turn". Our writing style was very different.

Aside from bunions and bad poetry Tom was unappealing. At least to me. I said I had an appointment and must go.

"Wait!," cried Tom, "I have some Armenian cucumbers for you."

Now Lorraine had already told me he did grow great cucumbers. Well, he had brought us a tiny sprig, which of course has to be planted. Unfortunately we have no garden spot on the fourth floor!

We all waved goodbye, (He never asked for my phone number), and he sped out of the parking lot on a flat tire – seemingly non-plussed over our encounter.

He still calls Lorraine to read her his poems – I wonder if ever I will find the perfect, or near perfect, man???

MVD (Motor Vehicle Division)
By Ellen Canterbury

To wait in patience is a virtue,

Given to a few

To watch humanity shuffling by,

Foreigners, families, youth, elderly

To pay a registration fee

On automobiles

Roaring on the freeways,

Polluting the air

Here we are lord

Waiting

NEWCOMER
By Ellen Canterbury

Do you adopt the land,

Or does the land reach out?

Do you say, "This land is mine?"

Or is it the other way around.

The land possessing you?

I like to think it is the land

That has adopted me.

OBSERVATIONS
By Mary Reeves

Until I reached my 70's I don't believe I observed a lot, certainly not like I should have. Oh! What I must have missed! Now I feel I observe and am curious about everything.

I noticed since I became "old" that younger people, even my children and grandchildren, simply tune me out. Example: This week my computer man was here and I said "it's supposed to be 80 degrees tomorrow". "Happy Birthday" he replied.

I find myself improvising when talking to a younger person just to keep their attention, but so often I see I have lost my audience.

It's only been since I moved to a senior home that my voice has meaning, but now I wonder if some of these old people are really hard of hearing or just choose to tune me out.

I will observe many things from now on.

OUT MY WINDOW
By Betty Turney

Little creature on the fence,

You sit serene yet in suspense.

Your costume just the thing,

Garbed in beauty summer thru spring.

Singing your song every day,

Viewing our world- oh what do you say?

Our silly antics must amuse,

Cars with bleating horns surely confuse.

Just a quiver or sigh,

And you're soaring safe in your sky.

But not any more little friend,

On human friendship don't depend.

We've stolen your sky and air,

Smoke, planes and bullets- how unfair!

Could this be our God's way,

Let's join our hearts and pray.

I think you have the key,

Except for man you're pure and free.

Is there a way for you,

To tell we humans what to do?

Rushing without a pause,

Expecting others to have no flaws.

Nature's way suits you fine,

With patience could we learn in time?

Share your secrets with me,

Help our world be serene and free.

OF MICE AND MEN
By George Gardiner

I have had my share of encounters with those fascinating critters... Mice! I was reminded of these occasions when the movie starring a mouse, "Stuart Little", appeared on TV last week.

Over a good many years I crossed swords with Zippy, Whizzer, Mercury, Eight Ball, and the Professor. I'm pleased to say I preserved and emerged victorious in each case... except the Professor. That rascal, but we'll get to him later.

Anyone who lives in a rural community has had a mouse or two, or six as an uninvited visitor. As I told Wilma when Zippy showed up one evening,

"It's a field mouse. They are clean little fellas, not like nasty 'city mice'."

Then went over with her like a rock in her shoe.

"That mouse goes, or I do," was her ultimatum.

So, what does a man do? I bought a nice new trap, the kind that when the trigger is sprung... WHAP! Exit mouse.

I baited the trap with a lovely bit of bright yellow cheese. It looked very tempting. Then I set about to out-smart the uninvited tenant. First I put the trap under the sofa. Three days went by, nothing. I kept moving the trap. Nada! Now and then we would see Zippy zip from one room to the other. Wilma would glare at me with a look that would melt steel. Then one day I changed the bait from cheese to a dab of crunchy peanut butter.

It was late on a Saturday evening; I was seated at my computer working on my column, suddenly the quiet of the room was shattered with a resounding... WHAP! No Zippy, no more.

Before you think I am a cruel killer of little mice, let me explain. A mouse in your house is an intruder and can be destructive. I once found an unfinished manuscript in the bottom drawer of my desk turned into a handful of confetti. Another discovery came when part of the stuffing from the leg of one of Wilma's dolls showed up behind our dresser.

With Zippy gone there was peace for quite a while. Then one evening Whizzer whizzed across the living room floor; Wilma didn't say any word just gave me that steel melting look again. Whizzer could really travel; do ten feet in under four seconds. I though I had him one night but the trap only held about an inch and a half of Whizzer's tail... oh, I bet that smarted. It took some clever moves on my part but Whizzer's demise came during the night of Halloween.

Summer and fall came and went until my next engagement. Mercury was a fine example of mouse-hood; large, sleek, and moved like a gray streak. The trouble with mercury, he was a mite short on the mouse moxie. The very first night I set the trap, along about midnight, WHAP!

Nearly two years went by until little Eight Ball showed up, He was a really cute little fellow. He came scooting into my computer room one evening. When he saw me watching him he stopped dead in his tracks. His bright little grape-seed eyes were filled with a look of, "What have I got myself into here?!"

"Does your mother know where you are?" I asked the tiny little guy.

With that, he did a one-eighty and vanished. And I mean he vanished. I never in my life saw anything move so fast. I was hoping half grown Eight Ball would go his own way but no, he had to try for a taste of peanut butter.

Here I must tell you I didn't toss these little bodies in the trashcan, no sir, I buried each mouse side by side at the southwest corner of our property. Four little graves, unmarked, unknown, with only the wind to mourn them, and only the rocks to remember.

Oh, the Professor? Try as I could, I never did get him, I guess he had a DSM Degree...Darned Smart Mouse!

REMEMBERING...
By Trudy Gordon

Doing Laundry

I remember helping my mom do her laundry with the old wringer type washing machine. First she boiled the water and used a stick to put the clothes into the washing machine. She then carried the heavy basket into the yard, after climbing about eight steps up the stairway.

Sometimes when we were hanging the clothes the line would break and we had to pick up the dirtied clothes off the ground and re-do the entire laundry again; -- or out of the blue it would start to rain, and we ran out to take all the clothes down and back into the house while they were still wet.

How nice is it today, we can do our laundry in all kinds of weather. I wish my mom were here to enjoy our modern conveniences. Now that I do demos, I often have samples of wonderful soap powders and softeners to give to customers to improve their laundry. The problem is the people usually won't try new products because they are happy with their own brand. Wouldn't this shock my mother?

An Encounter

When I was sixteen, on Friday nights I would go to our neighborhood theater with a girl friend or my brother, Bob. I always hoped that the young good-looking usher would be on duty to take my ticket. He was so handsome in his colorful uniform. I always managed to give him a big smile, hoping he would notice me. He didn't. Some Fridays I would be terrible disappointed when he was nowhere in sight.

Imagine my amazement when years later I would see him acting on the large screen in so many theaters around town under the name Tyrone Power.

Just think, this young man who was once an usher, was now a very famous person that I could watch in the very same theater where he first caught my attention. I learned years later that his mother ran a dramatic school in Cincinnati, Ohio.

Early Morning Surprise

Our daughter Mel, was taking piano lessons at the age of eight. Her uncle was her teacher. We were so proud and enjoyed listening to her play.

Early one morning, after Mel left for school, I was shocked to hear the piano being played. After all, I knew Mel had left for school. I rushed unto the living room, expecting to see Mel there, but instead, I found my young three year old daughter, Debbie playing all of Mel's pieces by ear! What a surprise to see our three year old playing the piano.

Our daughters were fine piano players, and Joe and I were so proud. However, all these years later – where did all the talent go? Not even a piano in the house. Maybe later, who knows.

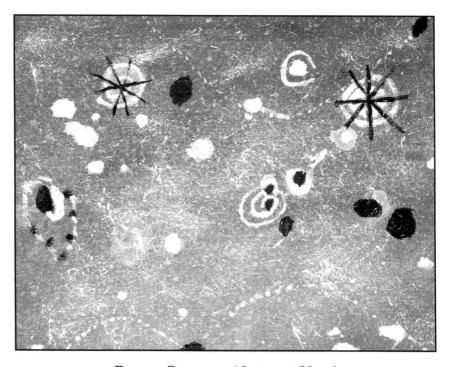

Penny Sarno—Abstract No. 1

PARKING SPACE
By Alvin C. Brewer

Look at the space you fill.
Are you incorrectly parked?
Doesn't it make you ill
That you're over the line?
Not parked straight this time.
Now, stop and pause.
It may not be you
That is the cause.
Perhaps it's the space
You're trying to fill.
As for me, I confess
The reason for this mess
Is I'm diagonally parked in
A parallel universe.
Isn't that perverse?
I wish the universe would
Get in line or
Maybe go in reverse.

SHOULDA STOOD IN BED
By Laura Lee McCoy

It was one of those days when I should'na got up.

As I turned off the alarm I stepped on the pup.

He let out a yelp, I fell on my knees;

Grabbed the only thing I could easily seize.

Pulled all the bed covers onto the floor.

I didn't mutter; I really swore.

Let out words unlike a lady,

(Some of them really quite shady).

Went to the kitchen to fix a drink

Spilled O.J. all over the sink.

Opened the box to make some toast

Aarrghh—there it was—last night's roast.

The pup wanted out, the cat wanted in,

The parrot contributed to the morning din.

Guess what happened as I opened the door?

Golden sunbeams flooded the floor.

Now who could be grumpy and blue

With all that sunshine cheering you?

Thank you, Lord, I really must say,

"It's gonna be a beautiful day".

THAT'S A LOT OF BULL
By Laura Lee McCoy

As a child I lived on a dairy farm just west of Littleton, Colorado. It was a typical dairy farm of that day. We had breeding stock, milking sheds, hay barns, a dog, cats and chickens. In particular I remember we had a big Holstein bull named "Ol' Monty" who was "Meaner than a junk yard dog".

One memorable day, my Dad had consented to loan Monty to a neighbor for a short time. Our neighbor Dan had an adjoining farm only a couple of miles away, so my Dad and Dan decided to walk the bull over to Dan's farm instead of trying to get the stubborn bull into a truck.

Monty was corralled a good distance from the house – across a bridge covering an irrigation ditch. Somehow Dad & Dan managed to get a rope through the ring in Monty's nose. This really riled him up. He pawed and bellowed and butted the fence something fierce. A board in the corral gave way and he was out of there. Dan was the immediate target of Ol' Monty's anger. From my precarious perch on the kerosene stove in the summer kitchen, I could see most of what was going on and Dan was running for his life! I'm sure those horns looked longer to him with every backward glance. At the bridge Dan took one last look over his shoulder and dove into the ditch right beside our biggest sow and recent litter.

Dad leaped onto the back of our old mare, Molly, and tried to rope the bull. With every attempt, Monty just shook the rope off his horns and kept coming towards the house like a freight train with a full head of steam. Mother came out to see what was going on and literally snatched me down from my perch atop the stove. The old bull was headed straight for the summer kitchen. When he hit the outside wall it sounded like thunder. The shotgun that was always kept in the corner fell over and discharged. Fortunately the shot went askew and only made holes in the wall. Ol' Monty was impaled by his horns just inches from where I had been looking out the window.

A very irate neighbor crawled out of the muddy ditch, and he was livid. "I wouldn't use that blankety-blank bull if was the last one on earth," Dan was heard muttering as he strode out of the yard.

Not long afterwards there was a major stock sale at the dairy; Ol' Monty rode away in a truck built especially for him.

SIMPLE PLEASURES
By Jeanne Nylander

I love good books and poetry
But only when they speak to me,
The complex meters I abhor,
I shun the mixed metaphor.

All verses, simple as can be,
Should reach the great majority
That grows with laughter, and love and friends
To reap such homely dividends.

THE FEAT OF DRESSING MY FEET
By Alvin C. Brewer

I was about to put on my socks

When I encountered a paradox:

Which was the left

And which the right?

The paradox was they

Were neither, but both.

Neither but both

How can that be?

It's an obvious paradox,

You see.

My socks are on

So now for my shoes.

The decision is clear,

No paradox here.

I've accomplished the feat

Of dressing my feet.

Isn't that neat?

THE GAME
By Joseph Apell

Let's you and I, thru Scrabble try,
Creating words, that hardly fly,
Telling ourselves, the game's the draw,
Not one another, I do implore.
So, play the game, and put aside
Those heart felt feelings, tis just pride,
Let's meet the challenge for the mind
For love is fickle and unrefined.
But, then again, with thoughts of you,
The game's a scam, it's you I view,
I'll play the game with great deception,
To win your heart, and your selection.

THE UNCERTAIN QUARK: Seeing Isn't Always Believing
By Charlie Stone

There once was a particle named "Quark"
Who spent much of its half- life in the dark.
And when you tried to discern it
You inevitably learned it…
Was never really there from the start!
It's the "Uncertainty Principle", they say
That makes it so shy in that way.
But reason alone doesn't half-way explain
How its unusual behavior's germane.
Well, I think that I know
Why the Quark behaves so,
And science should sit up and listen!
I think that it's best
If they gave it a rest
And stop worrying about nuclear fission
It's been prodded and poked
With one beam or another
'Til understandably it choked
And headed for cover.
It's not asking too much,
To understand that one touch
And the poor little thing will panic,
Run helter and skelter,
Try to seek shelter,
And hide in quantum mechanic.
And, one other thing
That might help us bring
The Quark some comfort and ease.
Call it "light" call it "dark",
Call it whatever you please…
Just anything but "Quark!"*
*(Just imagine our shame
If we had "Quark" for a name!)

TRIVIAL PURSUIT
By Frances McCreadie

Today was not a day of deeper meaning.

I managed only simple things today.

A cupboard door, one little chore for cleaning

And read a paper ere 'twas thrown away.

At ten o'clock I had a cup of coffee

And chatted with a neighbor for awhile.

Cleaned a drawer and found some missing papers...

A recipe that I had meant to file.

Today I did not do one thing that's clever,

I yearned for nothing as I swept the floor.

Could it be wrong to have no high endeavor

To be content with such a simple chore?

I dreamed and dallied and arranged some flowers.

Then watched a gopher scamper through the yard.

I wonder, did I squander precious hours,

Or did my batteries need to be recharged?

I do not know, dear God, if they were wasted

Forgive me for the time runs fast, indeed.

But thank you for the trifles that seemed precious.

Just for today that satisfied my need.

VIEWPOINT
By Alvin C. Brewer

So you have a view on the subject.
Don't smother it; take it out for air!
Express it if you dare.
But don't think anyone will care.
The land of viewpoints has become
The state of confusion
Where no one's opinion counts.
They lost the opinion scale,
All have equal weight.
I've discovered if I question my view
Before others do,
I'll prove less defensive or offensive
And open to you and your view.
It's safe to say, when we hold our view
Too tightly, we suffocate it.
Who knows, a willingness to let it go
May help us and our view to grow.

WORDS
By Suzanne Harvor

Squash

Sounds sick

And tastes even worse.

It makes kids object

And sometimes be rude.

When it appears for lunch

Even the dog won't help.

Send it out to the compost heap

Or, even better, call it something else

A squash called a rose

Might be delicious.

Wilda Hall—Still Life

WE ARE OUR SERENE HIGHNESS PAULINA—
Florid Witch Of the Southwest, and Secret Wife of the Wizard of Oz! Be thou wary lest a Flowery spell Be cast upon thee!
By Paul Norman

"Who in the world," you wonder, "Is this Paulina? Where ever did she spring from?"

She is, as advertised, the Florid Witch of the Southwest, and the serenely happy, although secret, wife of the "Wonderful Wizard of Oz." Paulina is also cousin of Glenda, Good Witch of the North, and of Nessarose and Elphaba, Wicked Witches of the East and West, respectively.

"How is that possible?" you ask.

Quite simply, Paulina is the sole offspring of the union of Harold, Glenda's uncle, and Maude, Nessarose's and Elphaba's aunt. Paulina has always stayed out of the mainstream, choosing to remain quietly, safely, in the background, out of sight of the people of Oz. Paulina almost always wears a flowered print dress with a full broomstick skirt, thereby able to ply the skies without the traditional cape and broom. Her favorite fragrance is Opium, a derivative of Poppies. She rarely, very rarely, casts one of her flowery spells, because usually she cannot predict how they will work. It seems Paulina's spells are controlled not by her, but rather by the heart of a person upon who a spell is cast.

Very early in her career as Florid Witch, she cast a spell that was so devastating to the recipient that she nearly died, a fate never ever sought by Paulina. That spell was so strong that Paulina couldn't remove it without help from her Cousin Glenda. As a result of that experience, she very carefully avoids casting spells unless she is absolutely sure the subject is of good heart.

She did, however, cast a spell upon her husband, the Wizard. He was not very forthcoming about his feelings for Paulina, so, knowing him well enough to be sure he is of good heart, she cast the spell of "essence of bridal bouquet" upon him, and they were immediately whisked off to Las Vegas where they married. This happened so quickly, they were never actually engaged; thus Paulina wears only a gem studded wedding ring. They agreed, afterward, to keep the marriage secret in Oz considering the Wizard was a major political figure there, and he feared marriage into the Witchery Clan might turn the munchkins against him.

I suppose you're wondering how they got from Oz to Las Vegas? They couldn't use Nessarose's ruby slippers because Dorothy made off with those when she returned to Kansas. You probably recall that she got them when her house fell from that Kansas
tornado smack dab on top of Nessarose, ending her wicked life. Being a Wizard,
Paulina's husband was able to fashion a pair of "transporter" rings which he and Paulina use, occasionally, to venture out of Oz. It is by using her "T" ring that Paulina is able to make her very first public appearance in the mortal world of Dorothy, as a jubilant
participant at the great and magnificent celebration of "All Hallows' Eve" at Fellowship Square in Tucson, Arizona.

Wilda Hall—Portrait Of A Lady

WHEN IN ROME DO AS THE ROMANS DO;
Usually Good Advice
By Charlie Stone

Three lads had vacationed in Rome
And had wanted, before they
returned,
To visit a historic cathedral,
But all three were very
concerned…

Since they knew not the language
Or, in the church, how to act,
They sought advice from a priest
Who gave them the information
they lacked.

"There's really no secret", he said.
"Just pay attention to the one
you're next to,
Stand when he does,
And when he sits down, so do you!

The three found their church
And they followed instructions.
They enjoyed the mass and
Found no obstructions.

They thought they had made it
All the way thru service,
When something occurred
That made them quite nervous!

When the man next to them rose,
All three stood up too.
It was then they heard laughter,
Why?...none of them knew!

The lads were embarrassed
And understandably confused.
So they asked the priest
What had the people amused?

And the priest explained
In his Italian accent
"That the parish had received
A most blessed event!"

And the priest further said,
With a twinkle in his eyes:
"I had just announced the baby,
And asked the proud father to rise!"

WHITE STUFF—By Gene Guerreno
The poet returns, home to Arizona, from a Michigan blizzard,
And the neighbors are informed that Snow
Is a mess! … and cold! … and Snow is WET!
Snow blows all over the place, getting set
To be obnoxious.
Snow quickly outstays its welcome and I say,
"The Hell with it!" and speedily slip away.
Furthermore ...Snow
Is rain in a foul mood that turns drops to drifts
And drops become icicles as each pretty flake sifts
Softly and treacherously past sweaters and scarves …
Small grandchildren become utterly sodden as one carves
The icy mess into a figure, with no time to admire
Before it melts, cannibalistically, into the mud and mire.
And finally ...Snow
Will transmute itself to a form of leaden billow,
That an idiot relative likens to a feather pillow,
Before handing you a shovel to remove little marshmallow
Puffs that, picturesquely, cover the road he says goes
To the airport. Don't you believe it! Snow blows
Copiously back, to cover the piteous bit that shows
Your labor has been in vain. The damnable stuff
Is back again and sensible people say, "Enough!"
And if I can get past that airport - maybe closed out …
And if the blessed airplane stays aloft and stout,
And if Arizona hasn't blown away in the desert wind,
I may never see another flake of snow … GOD SEND!
(And the Poet says, "It is, too, a Poem!")

CHAPTER FIVE

How High The Sky

Our minds, like our bodies, need regular exercising. The following pages reflect the results of this exercising.

To paraphrase Descartes; "We think young, therefore, we are!"

A CLOCK'S NOT TIME!
By Charlie Stone

Time is measured in many ways

By shadows case, and filtered sands,

By years and months and finally days.

By hours and minutes and second hands.

But, if clocks everywhere were to suddenly end,

Time would continue from dawn to dawn

To heal our wounds and continue to be

The "it" when we say that "it marches on."

And, just as a clock is not really time,

Religion's not really God, we'll see,

But simply a way of comprehending

An incomprehensible mystery!

As many religions as there are in the world,

There are just as many that say

That theirs is the only way to God

And that others will lead us astray!

There's no need to quibble where we are at odds,

And about those things that don't matter,

Just know the difference between sinners and sin,

And love the former, forgiving the latter!

ARE WE WINNING THE RACE?
By Charlie Stone
Did a cosmic sneeze
Set everything in motion
And then produce matter
That came out of the ocean?
And was there a moment
In the history of man
That he became aware
And proclaimed "I am!"
We've come a long way
From that humble beginning
And still have no idea
If we're losing of winning.
From hunting and gathering
To creating instruction
On how to make weapons
Of incredible destruction
Our history has been
A journey amazing
For developing things
Both damming and praising.
As science leaps forward
At a bewildering pace,
Our attention is focused
On winning the race
That rat race we're in
Makes us realize that
Even though we might win,
We may still be a rat!

BETTER LUCK NEXT YEAR
By Mary Reeves
Christmas came and went last year
I heard from those near and dear
If they had read my list and
Checked it twice – I had
Asked for things really nice

What I asked for:
High heeled boots
Bob Dylan's music
My own Golf Cart
First Class travel plans
Face lift

What I got:
Sensible shoes
Mormon Tabernacle Choir
City bus pass
3 nights in motel six
Pond's cold cream

ENVIRO CRISIS—DO WE CARE?
By Francis McCreadie

This world in which we live seems to be getting smaller, but its environmental problems are growing bigger. The oceans our only source of water supply, are slowly becoming one big sewer, but what if we ignore this and reach the point of no return?

There is definite global warming. Ice-locked northern and southern Polar regions are thawing to the point of possible flooding along the coasts of our land.

Oil exploration in Alaska is another subject. How would this affect the caribous' yearly migrations from Alaska and across Canada's northland? Do we need this when we are so close to having renewable energy? What about the huge hole in the ozone over Antarctica? These are big problems with no ready solutions. I care! Do you?

EXISTENTIALISM
By Charlie Stone

There once was a professor

Who taught about existential thought.

On his last day of class,

He told his students "to pass,

You must write what existence is about"

He then placed a chair on his desk, and said,

"You have 30 minutes to write

Why this chair's not here, but instead,

It's really nowhere in sight."

They wrote of all the knew

About the nature of "chair",

And just why it's true

That the chair was not there.

And when the professor announced,

"We're finished",

All the class remained there,

Undiminished,

Except for one who had already left,

Whose paper was actually best!

He had summed up concisely,

And phrased it quite nicely.

In two words with an eloquent flair.

He had written quite precisely:

"What chair????"

EXPECTATIONS
By Joseph Apell

With morning light I raise my head
To shed the comfort of my bed
I yawn and try to collect my wits
And thought involving delightful bits.
I plan to seek the company of,
The presence of a comely dove.
It's not my desire to be alone
Doing penance, and to atone.
So, with these pleasant thoughts in my mind
I plan my day and hope to find
Reciprocated expectations, joyful too,
And expectant love, that should ensue.

George Erickson—The Clown

FREE WILL
By Alvin C. Brewer

To what extent is our course set in concrete,
Poured into a mold not of our creation,
Fashioned by formulas held secret?
The forest has its edge,
The sea its shore,
The room its wall,
The house its floor.
Boundaries make them all.
How free am I to do as I please?
Perhaps like all of these,
The measure of my pleasure
Is determined by it boundaries
We'd be wise to confess
Our free will caused this mess.
The first exercise of our will was
To choose the limitations of its expression.
Does this mean my free will
Will choose not to be free?
Or is it just a ruse or excuse
To those who claimed it never was?
The concept of my free will may be treason
Caused by a rebellious reason
But even every reason has its season.
In conclusion,
The concept may be a
Product of my ego,
Just a dream or a wish.
My soul informs me
Only love is boundless.

GOD'S PALETTE
By Stella Klepac

Green is cool, and white is chaste;
And red is rich and rare;
Yellow's life and sunshine,
And little children's hair.
Lavender is twilight,
And orange is a flame;
Black is in the midnight –
But of all the colors you name –
Blue is my choice'
I love it best,
God must have felt the same…
For he put blue in all his skies
And in each newborn's eyes
And all the oceans blue…
To say nothing of forget-me-nots,
And phlox and larkspur too.
When God laid down his palette,
Of every other hue
A goodly quantity remained—
But he used up all the blue!

IN PRAISE OF THE SOUTHWEST—By Stella Klepac

Coming from the snows of the North,
It is like Fairyland.
That strange feeling of déjà vu—
Not seen before, but somehow familiar.

When you have experience the Southwest,
You never forget it—it tugs at your heart,

And draws you back,
You never again wholly belong
To the place where you were born,
Or where you lived, or were a child.

There remains a little lonesome spot
Inside you, that always remembers
The blue sky and the sunshine.

When we make it our new home,
We adore it; we detest it—
Our love for the West
Has the flip-coin ambivalence of any love;

How delightful in the spring, A riot of color and bloom,
When the early mornings are cool,
When the grass is wet under our feet
And the trees glitter In the light that is climbing the
mountains
And the mocking birds are going mad with joy,
Just because the sun came up.

The mockingbirds, proclaiming their passion;
Composers, each pouring out his paean of praise.

How we hate it,
In that Hades interlude
When Satan blows his burning breath
Upon us, and flings the dust into our faces,
And the palm trees are flouncing in the wind,
And the sunshine lies heavy on our heads—
A land too much loved by the sun.

Some run away to other places – to the mountains
or to splash and play near the water.

An eternity of sand and sun,
And then the benison of the monsoon rains,
Little by little the coolness comes
…And we love our Southwest!

JOURNEY FROM SHOWER TO THE EASY CHAIR
By Phyllis B. Amos
Two steps forward
One step back
Come on babe
You're right on track
Two steps forward
And – woops wobble to the side
Looks like this might be a bumpy ride
Two steps forward
Uh oh grab the wall
Its okay
You're not going to fall
Two steps forward
A small pause
Got your balance
Defy gravities laws
Two steps forward
Just one more
No you won't
Greet the floor
Two steps forward
Maybe even three
Here's the chair
VICTORY!

JUST A FEW WORDS ABOUT TUCSON DRIVERS
By Stella Klepac

A pleasant little city upon the desert lies,
Encompassed by the mountains, under endless skies—
The Old Pueblo's loveliness
Holds all our hearts in thrall,
But – the terrible Tucson driver
Is the deadliest of them all!

When the sun your head is frying,
Because there isn't any shade;
When to cross the street you're trying,
Comes the thundering parade.
An army! An army! A blundering brigade.

Vehicles – a varied lot,
From the tiniest in-and-outer,
To the charging juggernaut.
Drivers, too, of every ilk—
A bumpy ride, or smooth as silk.

Some are driving by the rule,
Skillful hands, alert and cool.
Some are good and some are better;
They do their duty to the letter.
Good, better, best,
We shall let them rest,
While we poke a little fun
At those who don't quite "pass the test".
Broadway is a speed-way; Wilmot's just as breezy.
35…45…57
But look at that sight-seer taking it easy
Drifting along at ten or eleven.

One-armed wonders are not a minority;
The left hand manages the auto,
Personal business gets the priority,
The right hand's doing what it hadn't ought to.

140

With her infant on her shoulder;
Or her doggie on her lap;
Or swooshing up her hairdo;
Or she's studying a map.

Or he's chomping on a Bosa,
And sipping up a cup of brew;
Or he's taking notes sub rosa,
While talking on the tele, too.

Some are traveling in twosome
And are chattering vis-à-vis,
With his girlie on his elbow,
They are slurping up their fizz,
For the thirsty Tucson driver
Is the busiest there is.

He blares his radio (no doubt about it)
As the car won't run without it,
Poor soul, without his BOOM, BOOM, BOOM.
His life would be inane.
Can't hear the traffic, can't hear the train—
The train? The train? He can't hear his brain.

He is rocking while he's rolling;
The vehicle is throbbing, the head, it is a-bobbing,
If his thoughts are somewhat scattered
And his steering is a bummer—
So what? The Tucson driver,
He hears a different drummer!

There she screams around the turning,
Just listen to that rubber burning!
She hates her tires, but loves her horn.
She beeps and beeps with great delight,
She beeps at everything in sight.

Her honking really gets absurd!
Yes—the tootin' Tucson driver,

JUST A FEW WORDS ABOUT TUCSON DRIVERS

Is the noisiest ever heard.
Why does a Tucsonan cross the road?

With a mighty jete, I'm on my way,
With winged heels I won't delay.
The cars are waiting, poised for battle.
Defensive driving at its best—
For those terrible Tucson drivers
Are the wildest in the West.

LOLA AND PAT
By Mary Reeves

What a bond these two had! Both lived on the top floor and would meet each morning on the walkway—greeting each other affectionately.

There seemed to be a need in both of them that was fulfilled by the other, and there was no way to keep them apart!! Lola, desperate to get to Pat would dash madly to her door to scream and wriggle until Pat opened up.

Pat would walk a lot, (hence that slim figure), and if Lola was not allowed out, she would alert Pat as she walked by, always on the table or looking out the window somehow. They would visit through the window.

Now I am not allowed to interfere with this love affair, even though I am "the owner" of Lola, (she probably prefers "roommate"). She is, however, a common housecat.

Then, sadly, Pat had to go away—the goodbyes between these two lasted most of that day—hard to witness! What memories each must have and what better therapy than someone to love.

PRAYER AT EVENING
By Stella Klepac

Thank you, Father, for the night,
The darkness, still and deep;
For rest and sweet oblivion—
The benison of sleep.

REFLECTED GLORY
By Stella Klepac

They say the moon does shine
On reflected, borrowed light,
Which she has captured from the sun
And does soften and refine
To suit the quiet needs of night.

THE COMPANY YOU KEEP
By Alvin Brewer

On the highways and byways of life,
A quiet mind and a contented heart
Are your best companions.
They travel light and
Bring you delight
With their gifts of peace and joy.
These gifts if fully employed,
Will lead you to the path of love.
Is there a better route?

THE COLORS OF ARIZONA
By Stella Klepac

Arizona is not brown,
Except to those who have not seen it.

We have every tint in the spectrum,
And a few shades and variations of our own.

The air shimmers golden-yellow
When the sunshine lies heavy on the landscape.

There is nothing on the face of this earth
That is bluer than the sky of Arizona.

That awesome azure softens at twilight
Into turquoise, lavender, and deepest indigo.

Green we have abundantly,
From the delicate chartreuse of the Palo Verdes
To the dark blue-green of the pines.

The very rocks glow ochre, orange, red, rose and blue.

Gorgeous canyons
With their kaleidoscope-ing colors.
A brilliant and constant display,
Changing, shifting, melting, merging—
A sight to ravish the senses.

Fat white cotton clouds drift and wander,
The snow, beautiful on the mountains,
The trees that bloom lushly in the spring—
Our early fervent spring, when
Budding, bursting, blossoming,
The desert's beauties are unfurled.

The scarlet flowers of the ocotillos,
Perched like birds, swinging in the wind.

The yucca trees, crowned with white,
The saguaros that lift their creamy circlets,
The smoke trees, like puffs of gray fog.

Millions of lowly things,
Happily flourish on the desert floor,
And peep out of crevices,
A lovely mosaic of purple, yellow, red, cerulean.
A riotous rainbow.

At sunset our scene may be glorified in fire—
Our sunsets make poets of us all.
The amazing colors of Arizona…

THE CATALINAS
By Ellen Canterbury

These are my mountains,
They have been given to me,
But I will share with anyone,
Who lifts his eye to the hills.
My mountains are blanketed in smoke
A shroud of mourning for man's folly
A match carelessly tossed
Has wreaked havoc on my hills
The winds die down.
The fire is out.
Once again my mountains
Return to peace and tranquility.
The sunrise finds each peak casting its shadow,
Revealing the contours of my land.
At noon the sun is high.
The mountains look less austere.
The shadows are gone
The canyons seem to have disappeared.
At sunset my world is lavender and mauve.
A muted splendor crowns the day.

THE MISSING TURTLE
By Ruth Spitzer

Robert Louis Stevenson wrote, "The world is so full of a number of things I think we should be all as happy as kings."

As a teacher, I was fortunate to be able to share new experiences with my pre-school students, and see the world through their eyes. The class was located at Temple Beth Shalom. Our room was located next to the room that held morning prayers.

On this particular day as the children were coming to class, Jennifer arrived with a caterpillar in a jar and said his name was Tippy. She loved him dearly. Tippy was placed next to Jennifer at her desk. Wherever Jennifer went she took Tippy with her. Jennifer declared that since she couldn't have a dog, Tippy was her pet. Jennifer's mother had found the caterpillar on a Mulberry bush and placed it on a twig with lots of leaves in the jar with Tippy. During the morning the children took turns watching Tippy munch on leaves. We had a short discussion on how Tippy would gradually build a cocoon and emerge into a butterfly.

After lunch, a kind person presented us with a box turtle with a wash basin for his home. We put names on the board for the turtle and voted. Now we had a caterpillar named Tippy and a turtle named Hermin. It was a bonanza day. Daily we watched Tippy and played with Hermin.

Everyday, Mr. Cohen would pass the turtle to go to morning prayers. Everyday he would mumble, "It's not kosher to have a turtle in a temple."

Slowly, Tippy became dormant and started to build his cocoon. Every day the cocoon became larger. Every day Mr. Cohen walked by Hermin mumbling, "It's not kosher."

Finally the cocoon was large enough to actually see the outline of the butterfly. We were enraptured with excitement. We put Tippy in the center of our circle and watched with anticipation. Sure enough, Tippy broke through the membrane and a beautiful yellow butterfly emerged. Jennifer was so excited that she immediately opened the jar and Tippy flew around the room. Jennifer was in tears. She wanted her pet. I climbed chairs, tables, cabinets and finally retrieved Tippy. We put him back in the jar and started to discuss his future. Our conclusion was that Tippy was born to be free and not live in a jar. He needed to find other butterflies. So we went out to the playground, waved goodbye and watch him as he disappeared in the wide blue yonder.

A few days later, Hermin, the turtle disappeared. We searched the sand box, and the cabinets. No Hermin. Finally Karen said, "Hermin must have flown away. He probably needs to find another turtle to play with." "Well," I said, "That's a possibility." The children said, "Yep!"

So if you see a Flying Turtle, it's probably Hermin.

TO DREAM
By Joseph Apell

I got to bed and on to sleep,

To expectant stages that are replete,

With hopeful dreams which consummate

Life's happiness in every state.

To find fulfillment for one's being,

Which escapeth one, in daily teeming,

An aspiration that's so profound

Giving credence for being around

But, having put myself to rest,

To high expectations of the best,

My dreams to dream are sort in vain

In timeless search and unattained.

I vow in desperation to uncover,

The ability, to discover,—

To dream.

TORTOISE WINS RACE WHILE THE HARE IS SLEEPING
By Toni Smith

I was entering my second week in the Stroke Rehab Facility, and feeling comfortable with the surroundings and daily routine. The morning started with the usual socializing among the inmates, positioning of the wheel chairs and walkers, and warm up exercises in what I called the "wreck" room. I was not looking forward to the tough task ahead of walking between the parallel bars. At that moment a young woman came striding into our area, and glanced at our group. She looked around, smiled, and nodded to me as she came closer to our circle.

"You are Toni?" she asked in a husky voice. "Yes," I answered, wondering what prompted this interruption. "Come with me."

I felt as if I should be saluting. I struggled from my chair to my four legged walker and wobbled across the room to a large, flat, low leather covered mat on legs which stood all by itself. It reminded me of a table in a Sushi restaurant, where people sat on the floor to eat the meal. I waited for instruction, not having the vaguest idea what to do.

"My name is Darcy, and I will be your instructor for this phase of your rehab. You have indicated that your goal is to be able to go to John Denman's clarinet concert at the Music Hall in two weeks. Your instructors have agreed to help you meet that goal, but it is going to take hard work on your part and complete concentration during the exercise periods." Darcy smiled, "Any questions?" I couldn't think of any at the moment. "No Darcy, not yet."

"Okay, what I want you to do is shimmy yourself onto this mat and slowly lower yourself to the floor, lay down, and then get back up onto the mat. Take all the time you wish, I'll be checking on you every few minutes." She walked away smiling. Ha! Slow is the name of the game. After what seemed an hour's effort I huffed and puffed my body from my walker onto the mat.

"Not bad." Oh no! Laying on the mat beside me was "Purple Rage," the little old lady that had been following me around since I discovered her in my bathroom mirror the second day after my stroke. We had become inseparable.

"Bet you wish this was a Sushi Bar now," she croaked, "Think you will be finished by lunch time? I don't like going into the dining room late so that we are the last ones to get served."

It seemed as if she were nudging me closer to the edge of the mat. I was almost to the edge, and ready to slide onto the floor. Whew! I think I am going to make it. I was down, flat on my back, huffin' and puffin' and looking up into the face of "PR", as I now call her. She was lying on her stomach with her head hanging over the mat, smiling at me.

"I'm right proud of you, getting down there in less than an hour. Now start getting back up here, time is marching on toward lunch."

I just groaned and let my bod' try to get up gumption enough to get back up on that mat. The longer I lay there the higher that mat seemed to be.

"How are you doing down there," came Darcy's cheerful voice. "Fine, just fine." I thought of other words, but my sloppy speech would not have done them justice. "You are doing fine. Just take your time, and you will be up on the mat and ready to go to lunch."

I saw Darcy disappear around the corner of the mat, which by this time must have raised up another foot, or so it looked to me. Now this is the hour, the time, whatever, to heave the bod' back up on the mat. I couldn't see "PR" hanging over the edge anymore and I wondered why. Back to the job at hand. With every ounce of energy I could summon, every grunt and groan I possessed, I finally could peek over the edge of the mat; however I was just on my knees. I heard a snicker. PR. She hadn't disappeared. I finally rolled my body up and over the edge and collapsed in a groaning heap on the mat.

I lay there virtually panting and sweating profusely. What was that noise close by, in fact right beside me. It was PR curled up on her side sound asleep and softly snoring. She earned her name now, Purple Rage. She wore the purple but I was in a rage. She couldn't stay awake to compliment me on what a great job I had done. And it was great, I ought to know. Oh well, the tortoise wins the race while the hare is sleeping.

UNDAUNTED
By Stella Klepac

Your arms are now my haven,
Serene from any storm;
Your love has made me dauntless—
I'm safe; I'm home; I'm warm!

Charles Stone—Birds Of Prey

VOODOO WOMAN
By Marion Brown

Voodoo Woman

With hooded eyes

Seeing what no-one else can see

Swaying, chanting

Weaves her magic

Forever cloaked in mystery

Flickering candles making all

Grotesque shadow on the wall

Voodoo Woman

Beats her drum

And tonelessly begins to hum

Head thrown back

Eyes unblinking

Charging face

Anther entity sits in her place

Words tumble forth

Loudly keening

A frightening message

Of special meaning

But – no one knows

And no one hears

As Voodoo Woman

To herself returns

And muses

On her "dream sojourn"

CHAPTER SIX

Shine Like The Sun

Ever so often you meet someone so radiant and beautiful that you feel your spirits uplifted by their warmth and compassion.

The stories and poems in this chapter have tried to capture that intangible quality that is so hard to describe, but so readily recognized.

A LETTER TO LENORE
By George Gardiner

I am a man among men when the day is full.

When the sun is pouring light on the green busy world.

I live in my mind by day, but at night my Darling,

I move into my heart and I remember.

I long for you and I walk into the night

Side by side with our memories, yours and mine.

The night winds are soft, like the light from a candle,

Like the music of your laughter,

Like the love in your eyes.

I look for you remembering your favorite flower,

Your favorite song.

Remembering our love, how you felt,

Close to me, in my arms.

I miss you in the darkness of a starlit night,

I look for you under a sympathetic moon,

At night, my Dear, I move into my heart,

And I remember.

A NEW BROOM
By Laura Lee McCoy

If the weather is cloudy and gray
And you're having a really blue day,
Pick up a pen and write 'em down,
Those pesky things that make you frown
You'll find as you sit and mope
And say to yourself, "There ain't no hope,"
Your pen won't write, your fingers won't move,
Your brain has shifted to another groove.
Those little things that seemed so big
Just aren't worth a fiddlin' pig.
You have a new broom, get it down off the shelf.
Get a grip on the handle and say to yourself,
"I'm sweeping these miseries right outa the door.
They can't bother me no more, no more."
Next thing you know you're gonna shout,
"Hey, that bloomin' sun just came out."

A VISIT IN THE DARK
By George Gardiner

"I'm a little late, Sweetheart. It has been so hot lately I decided to water the potted plants by the front door before I came to bed. The flowers seemed to be doing well; especially the one you thought was so pretty.

It's ten o' clock, but I don't listen to the news anymore since you have been gone. The days are so long without you, Honey. I try to keep busy reading or writing letters. I wish now I had let you teach me how to operate the computer. So many people speak of receiving e-mail. Last Sunday I started working on our photo album. I always said that when I retired... I didn't dream how many snapshots we had tucked away.

Sometimes just looking at the pictures makes me sad so I simply put them away for another day. The bridge group is after me to play again, but my eyesight is so poor I can't do it. The cleaning girl was here today. I love to see her; she's such a sweet girl. I also look forward to Hazel dropping by with my mail. Sometimes I can persuade her to sit for a little bit.

I nap quite a bit and I have tea and biscuits every afternoon just as we did when you were here. Well, Honey, there's not much more to tell you. I don't miss you like I thought I would because I strongly feel you are here with me. So, I'll be with you in the morning. Oh, and don't forget, tomorrow is our 70th Wedding anniversary!

I love you, Sweetheart. Good night."

DIANA
By Marion Brown

Shyly at first, she came,
As Princess of Royal Fame.
To discover,
She was just a pawn
Made for royalty,
To spawn.
Gave her country
Two Princes Bright,
Who reflected
Her loving light
And from her
Learned respect for all,
And to heed a call of need,
Wherever it might lead.
To untouchables
Shunned by society,
Unconditional love
She gave freely.
While dour royals mocked
And disowned her.
She rose above
Her marriage sham,
Emerging tall,
Forever Queen –
In the hearts of all.

BOB HOPE'S BROTHER
By Rosemary Sample

My affair with Bob Hope's brother was intense while it lasted. As intense as an affair can be for an eight year old girl and a boy a few years older. We lived in Cleveland, Ohio in a house that had a nice back yard and the boy lived in the house next door.

My brother, who was four years younger then I, had learned to ride his tricycle that summer. Soon he was peddling away down the street, when I was not available to mind him. So, my parents had a fence built around the back area to keep him in a keep me in-sie too. It was still my job to watch him.

I hated that fence. It had rough red pickets two inches wide with spaces between them about three inches apart. There was enough room to see out, but not enough room to get out.

One afternoon, a boy came to the fence and looked in. I rushed over to where he was and started talking. Talking was what I did best. In fact, I talked so much that I was often told to keep quiet. The boy listened for a while until I took a breath, and then he said, "I can tell you a story, but it's very scary. I don't know if I should tell you. You'll be very scared."

That shut me up at once. I didn't know if I wanted to be scared, but after a little while, I said, "Tell me." It must have been a wonderful tale, it was the first time in my life that I really paid attention to someone else's words, and that I was impressed enough not to interrupt. We sat down on the ground with the fence between us. I felt like the princess who was locked in a dungeon and a gallant knight was going to rescue me. My brother wandered around the yard and from time to time came over to see what we were doing. He was the guard who kept me from escaping.

After that first meeting, there were a few other times when the boy came over to the fence, but I looked for him everyday. When he did come there were more scary stories. One day while we were talking, my brother came over to our spot and made disgusting noises with his mouth while he rode his tricycle around and around. He was an embarrassment, a bother, and a nuisance to me. "Do you have a bother?" I asked.

"Yea, I have a lot of brothers," he said, "one of my brothers, named Bob is in show business and he is good. Some day, he'll be great." I thought about that, but I wasn't too impressed with brothers at that time. "Tell me a story," I said.

All too soon the summer ended, it was time to go back to school. I wasn't a very good student. The three "R's" took second place to talking with my friends. I failed deportment most of my first two years of grammar school. This year, third grade, all at once seemed interesting to me. Our teacher read to us from a book titled "The Wizard of Oz." She read one or two chapter's everyday. I had to learn to read well because I wanted to find out for myself what happened next in the story. We had books in the classroom library that we could borrow and take home. Now I could have my own scary stories, whenever I wanted. I soon forgot the boy next door. Now I can't even remember his first name, but I'll always be grateful to him for introducing me to stories, which led to reading, and which led to the love of books.

Bob Hope became famous and his programs, first on radio and then on TV were our family's favorite shows. One day I read a magazine article about his family life. He had lived in Cleveland, had several brothers and there was a picture of his early home which looked familiar to me. Hah! His brother was my boy next door.

I don't know if what I remember is all exactly true. I could try to research to find out. No! It's such an interesting story, why spoil a lovely fantasy?

HARRY TRUMAN
By Stella Klepac

He had greatness thrust upon him,
He did not seek it,
It found him; and we had him
When we needed him…
Just a little man from Missouri,
A little man of lofty stature;
A myopic fellow who saw far into the future.
An average face and a notable nose;
A soldier's stride –
He walked into history
With a flip of his cane.
He didn't know how to turn a phrase
And didn't excel at little chatter,
His speeches were marvels of honest simplicity;
But he knew how to compliment a Princess,
With aplomb and style and grace.
The man had humor, too.
A humor that snapped and bit!
There was spirit –
A sassy journalist
Was clobbered with the alphabet.
Advisers he had plenty, a country full'
Some recognized him and knew what he was;
Some thought they could do it better.
They stood in line to slander him
When, eventually, he fired Doug McArthur,
The nation's hero, the nation's idol.

Truman, steadfast, let the waves break over him!
Those terrible days,
When the world hung on the bring of disaster,
When the world was a prison of dread and darkness
Desperate decisions a president must make,
Heart-rending, unexampled, unprecedented.
He must have talked away his anguish
In the arms of his wife,
His unbeatable Bess,
Who stood beside him on sturdy feet,
And helped him to endure it.
He paid her tribute publicly,
Gave her a little gift of sovereignty.
And the war ended …
For everyday that was saved,
So many boys lived,
So many boys lived, who would have died.
And peace became his purpose and prerogative.
He towers among the Titans – Harry Truman.

HIDDEN FEELINGS
By Francis McCreadie

You think, because you do not see me weep,
Forgotten is our love of yesterday.
You chide me that my feeling are not deep.
Love cannot keep, you say.
Garbed in such frivolous array.
The blazing maple, like a funeral pyre,
Stand on the hills a bright, defiant crowd.
Do they appease the cruel winter's ire,
Clothed as they are in colored fire,
Wrapped in a crimson shroud?
Or does a burning candle know
It's flaming, hot caress
Consumes itself and does it suffer less
In such a tender glow?
But, I will never let you know my pain.
I smile and you will know my heart is light,
Flaunting a red umbrella in the rain,
Hiding my tears upon a kerchief bright.

IS THERE AN EXCUSE?
By Toni Smith

Pearl was a chubby little girl with curly black hair and big brown eyes. People always smiled at her, and said that she would be a beautiful young lady some day when she outgrew her chubby stage. She was around six years old. One day she and her mother went to the neighborhood market. Mrs. Brower, a neighbor, was buying meat from the butcher, saw Pearl and her mother, and called out, "How's that cute little Pearl today?"

"Fine," my mother answered, "Driving me crazy with wanting to go out and play. I have so much to do with bridge club coming tomorrow. Decided it was just easier to go to the market which would keep her occupied for a little while."

Pearl was busy looking over the penny candy and did not hear the conversation. On the counter near the jars of penny candy was a good size basket holding clean white eggs. Pearl saw the basket and wondered what the difference was between brown eggs and white eggs. Usually her mother bought brown eggs. She couldn't take her eyes away from those shiny white eggs. Would they taste different? Pearl went back to looking at the penny candy, trying to decide what she should but with her three pennies.

"Pearl we have to be going in a few minutes, so hurry up. I am going to have the butcher wrap up the meat now, and then we will go home." Pearl decided what candy she wanted, gave the grocer man her pennies, and took the brown paper bag he handed her. As she reached up for the bag, her eyes glanced at the white eggs. They would be pretty if they were colored like Easter eggs, she thought… She didn't have any idea about Easter, except coloring eggs, the Easter Bunny, and candy. Suddenly she reached up and took one egg and slipped it into the bag with her candy. No one was watching because they were talking to the butcher. She thought she would take one more in case she broke one. I'll ask if we can bring them back after we color them.

Her mother called to her, "Pearl, come along. It is getting late and we must get home." They started out the door. "Just a minute Pearl," Called Mrs. Brower who was still talking to the butcher. "Can I see what kind of candy you bought? I love that penny candy." Pearl looked up at Mrs. Brower, "I bought two banana ones and one licorice. See like the ones in the case," and she followed her mother toward the door.

"Well now, it won't take a minute and maybe if I bought some I might give you a couple more banana ones because you're such a nice little girl." Mrs. Brower reached down, and Pearl slowly opened the bag. Her mother stood beside her, ready to hustle her towards the door. "What is this?" Mrs. Brower said in a loud surprise voice, "Two white eggs? No candy?" "The candy is at the bottom of the bag, Mrs. Brower." Pearl answered in a shaky voice. "What in heaven's name are you doing with two white eggs in you candy bag Pearl?" "I wanted,…" stopping as she look at her mother. "Pearl, where did you get those eggs?" Her mother shouted at her. "I just, …" Her mother grabbed the bag out of Pearl's hand, and started toward the grocery counter. Mr. Brown, the grocery man, was now standing just on the outside of the counter, scowling down at Pearl. There was a few minutes of silence. Everyone in the store stared at Pearl in complete astonishment. Pearl was dumbstruck, she tried to say she didn't mean to do anything wrong, but she couldn't talk. Her mouth was dry and her eyes were beginning to get teary.

Pearl's mother said, "I am sorry, Mr. Brown. I don't know what to say. I don't believe she really meant to steal those eggs."

She looked down at Pearl who stood with her head bowed, and tears trickling down her cheeks. "Put the two eggs back in the basket, quickly! Mr. Brown, I really don't know what to say. There is no excuse for this child's behavior!"

She grabbed Pearl's hand and rushed out the door. All the way home Pearl cried quietly, sniffled, and rubbed her runny nose on her jacket sleeve. It was a long walk. Every time she tried to say something to her mother, her mouth wouldn't work, and she couldn't make a sound. When they finally reached the house, her mother told her to go to her room. It wasn't too long before her mother opened the bedroom door, and said she had to go next door to borrow some sugar.

"I should have bought it at the store, but you upset me so I forgot all about it."

When Pearl heard the door close, she peaked out to be sure her mother was gone. She then ran out the door, across the alley to where Mrs. Wakely, her favorite grown up friend, lived. Mrs. Wakely was almost like her grandmother. "Come in child, what is the matter?"

She held out her arms to Pearl, who ran sobbing to her and climbed into her lap. She blurted out the whole story. "Mrs. Wakely, do you have an......"the sobs drowned out the words. Finally she said, "Do you have an 'excuse'?" the word was distorted with Pearl's crying. "What did you say? Excuse? Whatever are you talking about?"

"Excuse for my behavior, my mother needs it badly. She told Mr. Brown that there is no excuse for my behavior. He believed her." The sobs doubled in volume and Pearl curled up into a ball holding on tightly to Mrs. Wakely.

"Shh now, Pearl. Let us talk about this. You know taking something that does not belong to you is wrong, don't you? Your mother was trying to help you by having you put the eggs back in the basket. This is one of those lessons we all have to learn. Come let me see if I have some white eggs that we could color." Mrs. Wakely found some white eggs in the refrigerator. "Look we can color these, take them to Mr. Brown, and explain to him about the eggs you put in your candy bag." Pearl looked up at Mrs. Wakely, "I'm sorry" she said softly. Mrs. Wakely smiled, "Pearl there is no excuse to be found, just understanding."

LIFE AT THE END OF A RAINBOW
By Charlie Stone

At the end of a rainbow there's no pot of gold…

There's an incredibly beautiful life to behold!

All the spectrum of colors from violet to green

Converge on beautiful things to be seen.

The brilliant beauty of a cardinal's color,

The unrequited love of father and mother,

The awesome splendor of a star-filled night,

The breath-taking beauty of dawn's first light.

The beauty of wonders so distant and far

That we seldom realize how great they are,

To wonders so close we take them for granted,

Like colorful flowers that someone else planted.

Sometimes that rainbow may be hard to find.

It's then you realize it's a state of mind.

That the wisdom we gain by growing older

Tells us beauty is within us, as the beholder!

LOVE IN COLOR
By Aileen S. Mercurio

They sat quietly together before the fireplace,

And the gentle, flickering flames traced shadows on her face.

He took her hand in his and touched it with a kiss,

As he whispered, "Thank you, Life, for bringing us to this!"

The time these two were sharing brought forth his Artist-self,

And, as she drifted into sleep, he took paint and brush from shelf.

"I must take this Love she gives me and give it shape and color.

I'll paint a tapestry of beauty like unto no other!"

So, brush in hand, he gently stoked with shimmering silver-blue,

And, stepping back, he softly spoke, "Yes that is truly you!

I know no form to hold your Love. It flows through space to me.

Its gift is like a summer breeze, so colors you must be!

I'll paint you gray clouds, sending rain, and lightning, flashing bright!

I'll paint you velvet night time, with stars of sparkle-light.

I'll paint you spring time fragrance of lavender and green.

I'll paint you Lilies-of-the-valley and Daisy hills, serene.

I'll paint you autumn, red and gold, with chestnuts on the ground.

I'll paint you wild geese flying high with horn-like honking sound.

I'll paint you summer's birdsong, trilling ever fair.

I'll paint you bees and butterflies, winging on the air.

I'll paint you white-tipped mountains, with icy slopes of snow.

I'll paint you drifting sand dunes, where desert wind does blow.

And these your life has known and you have made them Harmony,

And blended them with love and shared the gift with me."

MAKING A DIFFERENCE: OR ONE STEP AT A TIME!
By Charlie Stone

As I was walking by the shore one day

I saw a boy in an unusual motion

Picking something from the sand

And throwing it back to the ocean.

And, approaching even closer,

My curiosity increased.

As I saw it was a starfish

That he picked up and released.

So I asked the boy an obvious question.

"I see what you're doing, but why?"

"Well, if I didn't throw them back," he said,

"I'm pretty sure they'd die!"

"I understand your concern, of course,

But it's such an impossible task.

There are thousands of starfish on this beach.

Would one less make a difference?" I asked.

And the boy smiled as he bent down

To continue what he'd begun.

And said, as he threw another one back,

"Well, it sure made a difference to that one!"

When confronted with an impossible task,

It's easy if you just learn to take

One step at a time and you'll see

What a significant difference you'll make!

MY FIRST ICE CREAM CONE
By Ellen Canterbury

Even the word "ice cream" conjures up a hundred memories. Nothing could ever have been such a foretaste of heaven.

In rural Michigan, with the warm days of summer approaching, we know that along with the wholesale vans delivering produce to be sold in my father's grocery store, would be gallons of ice cream…The metal ice cream container was packed in an ice-filled padded canvas jacket. At the time there was still no refrigeration and generators were used to produce electricity. The ice cream sold rapidly at five cents a cone, and we also knew that at the end of the day the ice cream container was ours.

Each of us, armed with a tablespoon, would dive to the bottom of the tank and after coming up with a scoopful for an ice cream cone, it was the other siblings turn. Three of us made short work of the miracle of ice cream on a summer's day.

MY LOVE SONG FOR EVERY DAY
By Jeanne Nylander

I love you when you're happy,

I love you full of woe,

I love you sitting quietly,

I love you on the go.

Each time I count my blessings,

As I so often do,

The three top spots all read the same:

You!

You!

You!

MY VALENTINE
By Joseph Apell

Dear Ruthie,—it's Valentine's Day,

A time to tell you in many ways,

How much you mean to this old fellow,

Whose thoughts of you are not shallow.

I want to call you on the phone,

To make a date for us alone,

But you can't hear, you know I stutter,

I dread the outcome, I do mutter.

So here I stand before your door,

With heart in hand, I do implore,

To ask, to write or even sign,

Won't you be my Valentine?

ODE TO A DEAD POET
By George Gardiner

Your life was not your own, your wishes in vain,

It was your lot to leave poetry for the rest of the world,

As the water lily rises from the much and slime of a swamp, beauty of words and rhymes were to rise from the darkness of your tormented soul,

Till the day of your feverish death, you walked in pain and despair.

In loneliness you turned to the pen to write across the night skies of eternity the jeweled words of your impassioned fantasies.

Into how many caverns of weird wonderments did your mind journey?

How many hours of horrors did you know in your solitude?

What mystic words were whispered in your mind but never written?

The melancholy majesty of your words will live into eternity.

The world only had a glimpse into the silver sadness and dreamy dreadfulness of your short and shadowed life.

Now, Edgar Allen Poe, poet to the ages, it's your time to rest in your solitude.

ROMEO AND JULIET
By Stella Klepac

They loved –
And fate their joy denied;
They loved –
And for their love they died…
Two hearts that pledged their constancy;
Two souls together eternally.

THANKFULNESS
By Laura Lee McCoy

Hung up the washing, did breakfast dishes,
Then sat down and made three wishes.
Wish it wasn't so doggone hot
Wish I was an author of real renown
Who was feasted and feted all over town.
With autograph hounds all clamoring madly
As I'm smiling and signing ever so gladly.
Oh, well, frustrated as you can see
I'm still very thankful that I'm just me.

THE TOP OF THE HILL
By Laura Lee McCoy

Have you reached the top of the hill?

Are you at the end of your rope?

Is your life at a standstill?

Do you sit around and mope?

Have you reached the top of the hill?

Do you wonder what morning will bring?

Are you satisfied with the way you've come?

Do you still hear the birds sing?

Have you reached the top of the hill?

Are your legs getting weak?

Don't give up now, my friend,

Just reach for a higher peak.

Have you reached the top of the hill?

Are you still looking ahead?

Don't dwell on what might have been,

Bask in how great life is instead.

TO TUCSON
By Stella Klepac

Hey there…
Come on down-
Come on down-
Come on down to Tucson Town!
We've got it all –
You'll have a ball;
The Old Pueblo's loveliness
Holds all our hearts in thrall.
A friendly town, a festive town,
A place of jubilation;
A somnolent "sies-tive" town;
The sun is a sensation—
Best weather in The Nation!
And the air is filled with birdsong;
And the winter is short; the summer is long;
And the sparkling air;
And there's space and to spare;
…and see the stars
…and bless the benevolent mountains,
 Our glorious guardian mountains.
Where the skies are not cloudy all day;
Where it's Howdy, Howdy all day –
--Welcome Stranger—
Nuestro Pueblo es muy bonito!

TURTLE ON A FENCE POST: OR THE UNSEEN HAND
By Charlie Stone

I once saw a turtle that got me to thinking.

He was up on a fence post just sitting and blinking.

I thought of wonders in space distant and far,

And how seldom we realize how great they are.

And wonders so close we take them for granted,

Like colorful flowers that someone else planted.

And of the beautiful things that are most everywhere,

And that an unseen hand must have put them all there.

Why would that turtle provoke thoughts such as this,

Causing my mind to reminisce?

Then I realized what I should have all along known,

There's no way that turtle could have gotten there alone!

I had completely lost sight

Of that poor turtle's plight,

Being absorbed with the revelation I'd found.

But, my immediate reaction

Was an act of compassion

As I put the turtle down on the ground.

When we feel the touch of an unseen hand

Does it just inspire us or make a demand

That we pass it along and touch someone too,

Whether a turtle, another person, or someone like you?

CHAPTER SEVEN

Our Spirits Challenged

The higher we fly, the easier it becomes to transcend obstacles in our paths. Challenges that prevent us from seeing the writer within us, the artist, or simply one who appreciates and enjoys the talents of others.

The myriad of activities Fellowship Square has available to us gives us purpose and direction. It keeps us from "getting old!"

AN EXTRAORDINARY PLACE
By George Gardiner

Sonoita is "just 45 minutes from Broadway," 8111 E. Broadway in Tucson, that is. In miles or minutes, maybe; but in lifestyle and lay of the land they are decades apart.

This is a world within a world, within a world, within a world. It is truly a man-made oasis in the Arizona desert. Palm trees, slender and arrow straight reach skyward. A large pool with a submarine super-structure style waterfall highlights the center courtyard. The many levels of tumbling water sometimes seem to be talking, or laughing, or is it just the melodic murmuring of the sparkling water? Every long walkway, and there are many of them, is bordered with bushes or flowers.

Blooming flowers of all sizes and colors. Rose bushes that stop walkers for a moment to admire and have a sniff or two. There is a large, manicured putting green that will delight any golfer's heart. That's where you'll find me if I'm not in one of the five delightful swimming pools!

There are four large four-story buildings all facing the center court-yard. The entire scene reminds one of a South Sea Island ocean-side re-sort. For the freshness and dew-covered early morning beauty, this is the place. However, those folks who live in this retirement complex that we have met are "back-home" nice. Here we are all in the same regiment. We all came (over 600 of us) for similar reasons. No longer do we need to deal with the stress, work and responsibilities we successfully dealt with for so many long years. We are free from routine, clocks and must-do things. We know why we are here, mostly what the future holds and how to make the most of it. For all that we are simply grateful.

The dining room will rival most any hotel; spacious, cheerful, with unbeatable service provided by a bevy of the most friendly young people. White linen table covers, linen napkins, a seven-piece setting of silver-ware and padded chairs that one could fall asleep in. And the food (you order from a menu), all I can say is, it's superb.

Last evening, after finishing my dessert (crunch crust blueberry pie) I let my eyes wander across the room, pausing at each table for a

moment. It came to my mind these people, in years gone by, were a vital part of what made America a world leader. Now, the mounting years have brought an end to their chosen occupations. I thought of the wide-reaching knowledge, wisdom, and talent now locked away in their minds. One evening we shared a table with a very alert 92-year-old who had spent his entire life designing aircraft, both commercial and military. Another dinner pard'ner was a man who taught foreign languages to both civilian and military. And on and on, now they were
recalling a bit of their youth as I watched them at table after table, laughing, shoulder patting, and just plain enjoying the moment. That's the blessing of Fellowship Square, enjoying the moment with other old-timers doing the same.

Having the mind of a writer, I had one of my "what if" attacks. What if a magical whiffle bird flew across the room, and in an instant all these folk were young again, teenagers, swingers, jitter-buggers, be-boppers? What a party we would have! What a difference the passing years can make. Time is a thief with a clock in one hand and a calendar in the other.

Yes, I have come to believe this is an extraordinary place to take up residence. It is surrounded with beauty and built on friendship. In short, it is the gold in the "golden years."

Now it is time for our walk past the fountains, through the roses and along paths bordered with bright blooming flowers. Still, I haven't seen a roadrunner, or heard a coyote since we left Sonoita Meadows.

A SECOND CHANCE
By Sheldon Clark

The golf match had just finished and he got up to get a glass of water. Turning toward the bathroom and reaching the center hall he collapsed to the floor.

He laid there in a cold sweat, thinking, "Call 911". The cell phone is in the bedroom on the charger, so that's out. The computer can get 911 fast, but it too is out of reach in the back bedroom. The one remaining chance is the emergency button on his Lifeline, (which should be around his neck, but is hanging on a towel bar in the bathroom). Mustering up all the strength he could, he managed to reach a spot under the towel bar, but could not reach his arm high enough to reach the button. With an elbow in the side of the bathtub and one last lunge, he just happened to activate the button. Had he missed, this story could not be told.

Thank the good Lord Security came as quickly as they could and called the paramedics. The response was fast and they assumed the importance of getting him to emergency as quickly as possible. The ambulance driver broke all speed record to El Dorado Hospital. The last thing he heard before passing out was someone saying "Code Blue!".

This story is true; it happened to me on June 13th, 2004. I have been given a second chance; which you don't often get. I am grateful for the professional response and all of the subsequent support from my friends in Villa 4.

I cannot stress enough the importance of wearing the Lifeline emergency button. Don't take it for granted—it can, and did, save lives.

AND THE BAND PLAYED ON!—By Toni Smith

The temperature was hovering around 100 degrees. No breeze was alleviating the discomfort and dusk was descending swiftly over Fellowship Square. People were slowly making there way toward chairs set up on the grass in front of a stage; some waving paper fans trying to create a breeze, others sipping water from commercial bottles labeled "Spring Water". Looking around me, it was obvious the dress code for the evening was "loose casual". Talking was almost a whisper so as to keep all effort to a minimum. About the only sound to be heard was the hum of the air conditioner generator and an occasional bird flying to his nightly roost. Everyone was smiling and greeting friends. At the designated time the microphones were switched on, the spotlights shone on the musicians and the announcer introduced the "Original Wildcat Jass Band!" As the first notes wafted into the air, the spotlights went out. The musicians smiled, shook their shoulders and kept up the beat. Two figures dressed in Security uniforms appeared from the background and began checking electric cords and switches. "Praise Be!" the lights went on.

Foot tapping, shoulder swaying, hands slapping knees was in full swing to the lively music. One could see dancing couples on apartment balconies. Then the spotlights went out again for the third time, but the band played on. The two uniformed gentlemen frantically changed the extension cords, plugged one in here, over there, everywhere and Behold! The lights went on. The concert continued with wonderful recognizable music we all love. The applause was loud and appreciative with the occasional vocal responses. But, as the evening moved along the lights went out again and nothing would bring back their luster. Did anyone care? Not that I noticed. The musicians probably were more comfortable in the cooler semi-darkness with only the moon shining over their shoulders. The evening made very evident the talent and professionalism of the Wildcat Jass Band. Their interaction with the audience was great.

The concert was for the benefit of "New Beginnings for Women and Children" and donations were exchanged for tickets. There will be many happy children and women in this organization due to the generous outpouring of gifts and donations. Thank you one and all. It was an enchanted evening as the Band played on.

CHRISTMAS CHEER ...
By Toni Smith

... filled our Christmas stockings here at Fellowship Square. Decorations sparkled amongst the flowers blooming in the gardens while inquisitive Reindeer watched as we passed by. The buffets and Christmas goodies sprang up here and there, enough to satisfy everyone's holiday appetite. There were a variety of trips which included the magnificent "Messiah", "Gershwin's and their world of music", TSO Pops, Tucson Arizona Boy's Chorus, Luminaria Festival at Tubac, Tucson Desert Harmony Chorus, and the Christmas lights at Reid Park Zoo. Did you miss something? Sorry. These were off-site activities.

Events here at "The Square" were also well worth attending. Our "Toys for Tots" Concert was a big success as usual with 350-plus toys donated. Abundant smiles for children Christmas morning due to your generosity. The unplanned happened. It rained on our Concert. Woot, did it rain. Not to worry! All the Christmas elves from everywhere rushed hither and thither, moving this 'n that so by Showtime all was ready for great music with Joe Bourne and Friends. The audience enjoyed songs of Nat King Cole, Frank Sinatra, Ray Charles and other ole time favorites. The weather outside was frightful, who cared, inside it was delightful. Did you see Joe dancing with Louise P.? Smooooooth.

There were Villa Tree Trimming Parties, Christmas Parties, a special Chanukah celebration, the Villa Voices Winter Concert and various other get-togethers with friends. To you out there, from Fellowship Square -- we know how to celebrate and spread Holiday Cheer.

Now Forward —Our thanks to all who made this past year so memorable.

GREEN WAS IN
By Toni Smith

"Who threw the Levi's in Mrs. Murphy's chowder?"

"Not I!" came a gravely voice.

"Not I!" roared out a loud voice, very much louder!

We may never know. The answer was not available on St. Paddy's day at the Street Minstrel's concert. However, it was obvious that green was in, and jiggin' and clogging were alive and well. During one of the faster Irish jigs played by one of the minstrels, Paul Norman and another gentleman showed their clogging ability and won acclaim with loud applause acknowledging their talent. (I wonder if they have a relationship with 3-in-one-oil for ankle and knee joints.)

The evening was a mixture of singing and dancing old favorites, both Irish and swing tunes. "Cuttin' the rug" was clearly demonstrated to the tunes "Kansas City", "In The Mood" and a smooth rendition of "Begin the Beguine".

"Sure an' tis amazing". The enjoyable music that can be heard from just two instruments; piccolo and guitar or clarinet and guitar. The audience brought "Wild Irish Rose" to life in living harmony. A loud and lusty "Harrigan" ended the evening with a real Irish hoot!! As we wended our way out the door nibbling on shamrock cookies and sipping something green we could say: "Sure an' it was a very fine eve-nun".

REMINISCING
By Toni Smith

I can almost feel the rain falling on my jacket and making the pavement glisten under the low lights along the driveway. New Year's Eve. How fitting in the rain—washing away 2003 and welcoming 2004 with a fresh new start. I think, "How different this night was compared to a year ago. I was new here, just beginning to find my way, and all these faces were a mixture of the unfamiliar." As I helped with decorations, set table, and went over the list of those who were coming I felt that this was where I belonged. We all were going to celebrate "looking ahead" to 2004, and "letting go" of 2003.

The doors opened and it was party time. As the partygoers checked in with us at the door, I was amazed at the number of faces that were now familiar and how many I could call by name. Some even knew mine. These people had come to a party and were ready to have a good time, and for the most part had left their problems and troubles at home. The room sparkled with the reflections of beautiful sequined jackets and dresses. When the band began to play the dancers moved out on the floor. Greetings were passed to each other with a smile, or compliments, or just a touch on the shoulder from a friend.

Requests for favorite tunes were given to the bandleader who quickly responded, keeping everybody moving and happy. Soon the floor was "smoking" from dancers' feet with the hot renditions of Kansas City. A slow romantic Moon River brought out the waltzers to cool down the floor. Not everyone was dancing, but all were enjoying the music and wonderful appetizers provided by our "super chefs".

Our roving photographer caught the partygoers, some by surprise, some by request, and all in fun. As I look back on the evening there were some very special moments to remember. The bagpiper of Fellowship Square, Jim Stirling, at ninety-nine years dancing to a swinging version of Lady Be Good. A woman in a wheelchair being gracefully moved about the floor in time to a waltz, and the stately tango performed by couples who made it a joy to watch. There were broad smiles on the faces of those whose names were called as winners of door prizes. There were numerous ooh's and aah's from those who partook of the delicious goodies brought out later in the evening.

As the evening drew to a close I felt, "these people have a zest for life, they share and care for one another and it is a wonderful place to be." Bring on 2004! We took care of 2003, we can take care of you!

Charles Stone—Coming Home

"SOMETHING" IN THE AIR...SOARED OVER FELLOWSHIP SQUARE...
By Toni Smith

And it landed in the middle of our "All-American Celebration Party." One could feel its presence as people lined up in the heat, smiling, greeting one another, forgetting all the world problem, their ailments, frustrations, and disappointments. It was time for friendship, enjoyment and letting our spirits rise to the occasion. The sound of the vigorous singing of patriotic songs almost drowned out the Swing-Thing band. Looking around at the decorations; flags, balloons, and center-pieces, one knew this was the Fourth of July. The people dressed to fit the occasion, red, white and blue or variations thereof. The participants came prepared to dance, and dance they did, from Country to Rumba to the Polka.

During the singing of America the Beautiful, I was looking around and wondered if others were like myself, remembering past Fourth of July's. I was thinking back to Chicago when I was a little girl, how excited I was about going to the park for Fireworks. We had to walk, because we didn't have a car. When we found a space to put our blanket down, I would look around to see if any of my friends were there. Most of the time there were just too many people, and my parents were afraid I would get lost if I wandered too far from our space. We didn't have any snacks during the long waiting period, so I just watched people. It was always hot and humid. After what seemed forever, the air was filled with thunderous explosions and the sky was filled with bril-liant twinkling sparkles, which dissipated and disappeared as they fell into space. After the long walk home, we enjoyed a big dish of ice cream on our screened-in back porch. It was quiet now, the excitement over and time for bed, but there was one last thing I anticipated. Looking up at the sky I waited and waited. Finally I shouted, "Look there comes one."

A single, lighted hot air balloon silently stealing across the sky. Where did it come from? Where was it going? Does anybody see it but me? Later, as I fell asleep I pretended that someone was waving to me as the red flow of the balloon drifted out of sight.

Drifting back to reality, I knew we didn't need fireworks for our celebration. Even though we are a cranky bunch sometimes, that "something" is a positive presence here and will keep our lives fervently passionate about living.

THE BUSY LEPRECHAUNS
By Toni Smith

The Sunday noon hour in our dining room was crowded with the usual church crowd and visitors enjoying a wonderful dinner with all the trimmings. Four and a half hours later the room was a hub-bub of activity with a group of lively leprechauns preparing for our St. Patrick's Day Party. The doors opened at five-forty-five so time was of the essence.

Clad in green for the most part, these leprechauns were busy decorating tables, setting up a table for a variety of sandwiches and hot appetizers, green punch and cookies. Soft drinks and beer were placed in ice filled tubs ready for the taking. Around the room shamrocks were being strung over the doorways, and balloons placed in green containers on the tables. The balloons swayed back and forth with the whir of activity.

The stage was becoming occupied with the musicians, wearing bright green bow ties, and warming up on their instruments. Outside, the weather was perfect and people were lining up, ready to "Party". It was time! The music was great and the dance floor was never empty while the band was playing. A march to the Irish tunes got everyone in the mood followed by a line dance, a rumba, swing and jitterbug. What more could you ask for? Those who didn't dance enjoyed the company and congeniality of friends and the party atmosphere. The food table was soon empty, proof of savory vittles.

"Sure'en it was a grrreat party, and the food was a wee taste of heaven, 'twas a wonderful time we all had. " Thanks to all you leprechauns, wherever you are.

K:

UNDER A CASINO SKY
By Toni Smith

It was early evening and about time for our outdoor concert to begin. The smell of blooming Gardenia's in the air and roses of all colors surrounding a pool with a bubbling fountain, added a Hollywood touch. There were chairs set up on the grass in front of an elevated stage on which the "Catalina Players" were setting up and tuning their instruments. Butch Bryant, accompanied by Joanna Spence, Leslie Boll, Amber Lee Harrington, and Megan Austin opened the program with a group of songs from Broadway musicals.

Numbers from "Pygmalion", "Fiddler on the Roof", "Music Man", "Sound of Music", "My Fair Lady" and many others transported me back in time to the Broadway stage and Hollywood musical extravaganza's of years ago. Solo performance by members of the group were all well done and enjoyed by the enthusiastic audience. Meg Austin, the youngest member of the group, seventeen, had a beautiful voice and received bounteous applause. We all felt this young lady had great promise for the future.

As I listened, I looked up, and was amazed. It was reminiscent of a Casino Sky; Cobalt blue with long streaks of white clouds tinted a bright pink from the setting sun. The tall Palm trees around us were like grand sentinels guarding the premises; waving their stately branches lightly in the breeze.

After the intermission, the second group started their program with a smooth rendition of "The Way You Look Tonight", with Julie McCrea, vocalist of the "Misbehaving" instrumentalists. Again, the music triggered many memories. The dancers in the audience were on their feet, not happy with just sit-down tappin' but up and doin' it. There were "swingin" couples on sidewalks, apartment balconies, and any available area for dancing. Occasionally there is an unexpected twist that appears at our outdoor concerts. That night: a "free spirit" in the form of a young woman whose "spirit" motivated her to create her own mood. An unplanned, but whimsical addition to the concert which reminded many of us what we did, and could do in the "good ole days". "Misty", "Moonglow", "Mack the Knife" and the finale, "Satin Doll" were stunningly played by Chris Dansdill, guitar, Sean Thronhill, drums, Ron Zastaury, string bass and Rob Resetar, keyboard. We wended our way home as the melody of "Route 66" faded into the night.

George Erickson—Wedding Portrait

WHAT'S BREWING
By Toni Smith

For months we have been the recipients of spewing fumes from the bilious broth boiling in our political caldron. We know the witches, gooks and goblins will be our there spouting and shouting, but we are going to out-spook them with our Halloween party.

As darkness descended, Halloween night, the bright lights illuminating the door to our dining hall attracted the attention of a band of witches breezing by on their broomsticks. They swooped down for a peak and were impressed by the costumed crowd streaming into the hall. They joined the crowd and parked their broomsticks in the corner. The table of appetizers tweaked their appetites, and the smooth dance music made their witches hats twitch. Spreading out through the room they joined in the revelry.

Soon it was time for the traditional costume parade to the tune of "The Saints Go Marching In". "Great! My kind of music," said one witch to the other. "Whee!" said another witch, "Look at those vintage vampires. Winners in my opinion. See Mr. Dracula? Looking for volunteers, I betcha. Looks lonely though." "Who is that little one bobbin' about in the habit, and the Orphan Annie look alike behind her? Special ticket to get in?"

The parade moved around the tables through the dining hall giving everyone a chance to admire the clever creative costumes. Snaking past one table, one witch whispered to her companion, "Wow! Who's that tall redhead swishing her shoulders?" "That's Tootsie. Coool, isn't she?"

As the evening wore on it was obvious the witches were enjoying the party. When offered more punch and cookies, the witches politely refused saying their broomsticks were twitching in the corner. Time to leave. Before their departure they went up to Mr. Scarecrow and Mrs. Pumpkin and wished them a Happy Halloween. "We hope you'll remember us next year. This is our kind of brew, include us when you start stirring up next years batch."

Mr. Scarecrow waved his cornstalky arms, and Mrs. Pumpkin smiled as they watched the broomsticks and passengers disappear into the night. Cool brew!

WINDS OF CHANGE
By Toni Smith

Everything is ready for the Luau! The tent, the food, the decorations, and the people – are more than ready. Everyone is milling about the tent entrance, waiting their turn, each with a ticket in their hand. This is a congenial group, smiling, conversing with friends, looking forward to an evening of good food and entertainment. Overhead a darkening sky, thunder rumblings, and menacing streaks of lightning were signs of a different scenario about to begin. A whisper of a breeze stirring the surrounding trees and ruffling the edges of the tent was even a greater omen of coming events. Within minutes the breeze became a wild wind roaring across the area, the thunder increased to crashes and rain came down in huge plops. As the wind increased, and the staff struggled to keep the tent from becoming a flying monster, a voice roared above the winds—"Everyone to the dining room! Now!"

Camera! Action! That was the impression all around us. The main performance began. The crew went into action moving all the props into place without missing a beat. As the people filed into the dining room, the staff cleared tables of linen and silverware, replacing them with colorful napkin wrapped tableware and decorations. Food appeared on serving tables arranged so people could be served from both sides. The buzz of people concerned about the whole show were now quietly talking and watching the efficient surge of activity going on around them.

Everyone was seated. There was an undercurrent of excitement as the audience realized it was curtain time. As people got in line and helped themselves to the sumptuous buffet, they all realized just what had happened in the past half- hour to forty- five minutes. A wonderful show had been performed by a marvelous crew of hardworking young men and women, strictly for us. The wind had changed everything that was so carefully planned, but offered us an unusual opportunity to say "Thank you, we appreciate every one of you." We residents of Fellowship Square are resilient and flexible and certainly appreciate a good show.

Ann Mari Brandt—The Farm

George Erickson—Renaissance Man

Wilda Hall—Home In The Hills

Arlene Radek—Feeding The Geese

Penny Sarno—Sunflower

Charles Stone—Flamingos By Moonlight

Bernice Steinhauser—Cactus Flower

Evelyn Wilson—The Red Barn

Charles Stone—The Puffins

Charles Stone—Roses

Charles Stone—Wings Of Eagles

CHAPTER EIGHT

Reflections From On High

As the song goes: "Thanks for the memories..." So the following pages capture precious moments of our past, worth preserving for the future.

24 FUZZBALLS ALL IN A ROW
By Toni Smith

Carrying a dust pan and broom in one hand, and a cup of coffee in the other, Julie stepped out on her patio, "Where do all these little sticks, pieces of grass, bits of string, and stuff come from? I just swept this patio yesterday, and here it is all back again," she muttered to herself. She looked over in the corner, as she set her cup down on the table. All the mess had accumulated near a large wicker basket. She sighed and began sweeping. From behind the basket came a quail clacking like a castanet and waving her topknot in an agitated manner. Julie stopped her sweeping, stood perfectly still and watched the quail pace back and forth in the front of the basket. After more clacking and packing, Mrs. Q reached down and scooped up several pieces of the grass, jumped up to the edge of the basket, poised there for a moment and then disappeared over the side.

"Well, that's a surprise. How did she get in there? That basket is tall with several big rocks in the bottom so that the wind won't blow it over, and fake sunflowers are stuck down in between little rocks on top. Not too comfortable or cozy, I wouldn't think!" Julie stood still and watched Mrs. Q bounce up on the basket rim, jump down, pick up more "debris", jump up and back into the black pit of the basket. After several minutes Mrs. Q decided to take a break and flew off to rest on the brick wall surrounding the patio. Still not moving, Julie waited, and after Mrs. Q flew away, she peaked into the basket. She had to move the sunflowers around to see inside. A rather large nest was squeezed down among the rocks. It was too dark to be able to see all of it, but Julie was astounded. "She has to work very hard to get all that material down there and shaped into a nest. I wonder how long this has been going on? Bill and I have been in and out of our sliding glass door many times and never noticed any unusual activity, let alone a Quail so close to our house!" Julie took her broom and dust pan, hooked her finger around her cup which she'd left on the table and went into the house, closing the door quietly behind her leaving all "nest mess" for Mrs. Q to retrieve at her convenience.

After what seemed weeks of waiting, peaking into the basket, counting and recounting eggs, the final count was 24. Was the count accurate? Who knows, but now her concern was when and if these eggs all hatched, how would they get out of the basket? Another problem was how they would get out of the patio area with a brick wall and an iron gate. These questions were all very obvious one morning when Julie looked out on the patio and saw Mr. and Mrs. Q frantically pacing around the basket. The castanet clacking was loud and piercing. She carefully opened the patio door, stepped softly out on the patio so as not to frighten the agitated birds. Bill was right behind her and they both looked at each other wondering what to do. Bill decided without conversation how to act, and slowly walked over and peaked into the basket. As they started to push the sunflowers to one side, they realized that there was a lot of a little clicking sounds,
and movement at the bottom of the basket. Bill took hold of one side of the basket, motioning Julie to do the same on her side, and they slowly tipped the basket on its side. Luckily the rocks were wedged tightly so they did not move. Mr. and Mrs. Q were clacking and skittering around our feet staying close to the basket. When the basket was safely on its side, Mr. Q became frantic and with one big whoosh of his wings, flew up on the patio wall and Mrs. Q was scurrying around the patio yard.

For a few moments, nothing happened. Mrs. Q skittered and scurried about, clacking, her top knot's jerky movements becoming more noticeable. "Will they attack us?" Julie whispered to Bill, who shrugged his shoulders. We looked down at a slight movement at the edge of the basket. There appeared a walnut sized furry fuzz ball with tiny feet and a tiny top-knot wobbling out of the basket. As we watched and tried to count these wobbling walnuts, they scattered out into the patio yard. Mrs. Q kept up her castanet clacking, and led the parade toward the gate. Oh! The Gate! Mr. Q proudly strutted back and forth on the wall keeping a sharp lookout for Mr. Roadrunner, who would love to view this parade. As Bill edged toward the gate, the fuzz balls kept in a scraggly line behind Mother Q. But now the little rebels were beginning to show their independence, and here and there a wobbly fuzzy one would veer to one side and start off in the opposite direction. No amount of clicking and clacking seemed to have any affect. I had sneaked over and opened the gate. The "walnuts" were flopping, bumping each other, turning upside down, then right side up, any way to get over the little step in front of the gate to the world beyond and safety. While Bill tried to herd the frantic scurrying rebels into the line, I watched Mother Q proudly march the rest of her brood to a large prickly pear plant into which all the little fuzz balls disappeared. It was quiet. Papa Q finally joined Mrs. Q under the prickly pear after all the hard work was done. But wait, what's that clicking sound behind us? Oh no! Here was the last little fuzz ball with his beak and head caught between the gate post and the wall, stuck tighter than a drum, going nowhere with all his flopping around. Bill carefully pulled him free, and pointed him in the right direction, but the fuzz ball had other plans. Clicking and clacking his little top knot a flippin' and flappin' he went "his way" into the great world of beyond.

We wondered if that was the 24th one? Where did he go?

AFTER THE RAIN
By Stella Klepac

Those red-vested character

Out on the grass

Are surely holding a convention.

Those seed-stealing malefactors,

Milling en masse—

Robins of every known dimension.

What a racket – and what a dither'

What a rushing, hither and thither!

Darting and dashing,

Gathering in swarms,

Flapping and thrashing,

And haggling over worms…

Did you ever see so many robins?

A VISIT TO THE LAZY RR
By George Gardiner

The morning breeze was a bit chilly as I pulled onto the dirt road leading to the lazy RR holding pen. I was in for a mighty interesting morning. The sun had not made it over the mesquite-studded foothills of the Santa Rita Mountains.

A stream of blue smoke curled over the croup of cowboys squatting on their heels around the fire pit in the center of the fenced-in arena. "We're wasting daylight," the foreman called out, "Let's burn em." The men tossed their smokes into the fire, pulled on gloves and headed for the action. It was branding time on the Lazy RR.

There were three branding irons lying side by side with the big "R" resting in the glowing coals of fire. The fragrance of the mesquite wood smoke floated all about as the first streaks of the morning sun rose over the nearby hills. I was there as a guest to witness my first branding operation. As I took in the scene before me, the thought came, "What a painting this would make, an oil on canvas no less."

It would truly take an artist to capture the colors. The canopy of blue-gray smoke, the green of the surrounding trees, the many shades of the horses, the shine of the polished brown of the saddles, the worn and faded shirts and Levi's of the cowboys, the deep red and white color of the cows and calves. And most particular, catch the glowing red of the branding iron and the sudden puff of smoke as the hot iron burns the hair on the calves' rumps. Ah, to be an artist and see what I was seeing on this brisk autumn morning. The men on horseback, the ropers, have the knack of "heeling" the calves. They pick a calf from the herd at the far end of the pen, and with unfailing expertise, toss the loop of their rope in such a manner it somehow hits the ground at the hind feet of the calf, scoots under and with a tug on the rope the calf is roped. Immediately it is taken to the branding fire. Two strong men known as "flankers" pin the calf down and position it for the man with the sizzling hot iron. Poof! And in an instant the calf is inoculated, castrated, and dehorned if there are apparent buttons. The flankers release the little fellow and he trots to his mother as if nothing happened. By then, another calf is at the spot of branding.

On this particular day, there were two ropers mounted on beautifully groomed horses. The horses are trained to respond to the knee signals from the ropers. Watching the ropers and their slithering ropes is nothing short of fascinating.

The entire branding operation moved rapidly, the dust rose to join the smoke, the fragrance of the mesquite – fire mingled with the sharp, pungent odor of the burned hair. I had taken a seat on the top rail of the corral to better observe the branding scene.
I was anxious to capture in my mind what my eyes were seeing.

As the morning's branding came to an end, the fire was doused, the paraphernalia gathered, then the men, laughing and chatting, headed for the black coffee and doughnuts in the back of a pick-up parked near by. In my writer's mind I heard the song of the West, a melody I have heard often, many times before. It is the creaking of saddle leather, distant bawling of cattle, the bark and howl of coyotes, the squeak of a windmill, the cry of a night bird, a cowboy's melancholy harmonica, all theses sounds and more that blend into the anthem of the West. Have I ever heard this ballad? As sure as you are reading these lines. In the shadowed dusk of evening it is there for all to hear. Of course, only a westerner can hear it.

It is a shame that the good days of life on a ranch are slipping into oblivion. Who wouldn't like, this very night, a thick steak cooked outside over mesquite coals, rare, tender, and juicy, with biscuits, honey and a bowl of margaritas, along with western music to dance to, as it was long years ago?

I attended such an affair on the Buenas Aires Ranch some thirty-five years ago. The memory is still with me.

The modern demand for houses has raised the value of land so high and the price of beef has not kept pace with the economy, creating a situation where ranchers have little choice but to sell.

Therefore, the huge earth moving machinery is slowly but surely devouring the grazing land as well as a life-style that will not be seen again. I'm grateful I saw a bit of it!

ALONE BUT NOT LONELY
By Mary Reeves

For most of us living alone in a senior home is a first. We went from home to husband without ever living alone.

In spite of being such a closely knit community, the activities provided for us and even sharing a table at dinner, some still remain alone and lonely. We suffer many emotions at finding our self alone – loneliness, confusion, helplessness and even guilt at being so comfortable and even enjoying the aloneness.

My husband and I had always fantasized about "Living in Villa Serenas" (Before it was Fellowship Square) – we stayed here many times on vacation from Texas, and moved back ten years ago when we determined he would no longer be able to travel. He got progressively worse with Parkinson's disease and soon became housebound, then bedfast. We still had a few laughs about "moving to Villa Serenas" and blaming our cat Lola for not being able to. At that time, Villa Serenas, would not accept pets.

After my husband died I lived a year in our home; everyone said I should – and neighbors not being what they used to be, I became very lonely. By about the third month I was staying in my robe or sweats all day! A friend and I got together and just decided we would make the leap—sell our homes and move here.

I have enjoyed my year and a half here a lot, met new friends, learned I have to keep a good attitude, get up, get out, participate and enjoy!!

AS TIME GOES BY
By Frances McCreadie

When I was small the future seemed so very far away

I didn't see how I could wait until next Christmas Day –

But now that I am older – the way it seems to me –

I almost think that the months are shorter than they used to be.

Can all these years have come and gone?

We cannot bring them back.

Can all those reels have been unwound

Then stored upon life's rack?

Those years have fled

How time has sped

It runs a speedy track

Like – going in the front door,

Sitting down and out the back.

If someone has the answer I would really like to know

Does the hourglass run faster the older we grow?

DOWN SIZING
By Ellen Canterbury

Everything becomes compacted
1600 sq. ft. becomes 600.
Wardrobes shrink to what is needed
Book collections grow smaller.
Food stocks have disappeared
Only All Bran, prunes, prune juice
One cannot live without.
Gone are the daily needs
Of flour, sugar, shortening
The makings of an earlier life
Of cakes, pies, and pastries,
All are no longer necessities.
Life is simplified.
Or are we suddenly rushing
Around to fill our days?
Fearful lest we lose ourselves
In loneliness

HOUSEWIVES AND POETRY
By Jeanne Nylander

My day had been long so, to break the routine,
I thumbed through my favorite magazine.
A verse caught my eye so read eagerly,
Only to find it meant nothing to me.
I turned all the phrases around, referred
To Webster or Wagnall for every word.
Completely exhausted and discontent
I finally realized what it meant!

LAMENT
By Frances McCreadie

A broken shard is buried deep,
Deep in my heart a-main.
And lest I bring it forth to weep
Fain would I let it lie asleep
To ease me of my pain.
But I the folds uncover lest
The memory ever wane.
To let it be I cannot rest
But hold it closer to my breast
To prick my heart again.

LIFE IN TEXAS – THE EARLY YEARS
By Mary Reeves

The journey from Red River County near Clarksville in Northeast Texas (where Mary was born) to the little community of Greenville took place in 1929. The 70 mile trek was made in only fourteen hours in the "almost" new 1928 Ford. Dan bought the car with the money he got from selling Belle and Rhoda – his beloved team of mules. He would not be needing the mules, as he was leaving the farm for good.

Mary was only three years old and did not actually remember the trip, but it was often talked about during the next years. This would be the first time Dan had tried anything but farming, and he and Ethel were a little reluctant to leave the family and be on their own in the "big" city. Momma (Ethel) packed a lunch for the trip – I'm sure there were red beans in a fruit jar, cold biscuits and sausage, cheese and crackers. Dan was thirty years old, Ethel only 25. Ivan was almost nine, Odis seven.

Even though it was the depression time, Dan had heard there might be work on the L&A railroad as a lineman, and he indeed landed a job there the very first day after getting to Greenville. He kept that job for twenty-eight years. Sometime later, the Ashley's, Ethel's kin, also moved up to Greenville. Our first house, "the big yellow house", was located next to, or backed up to the railroad.

We never actually owned a home those first years, and also some-how lost our nice car. We were three miles from town and school, but all of us walked, and even came home for a good vegetable hot lunch!

One early joy of childhood was "dressing up" on Saturday and walking to town with Momma. We would have an ice cream, go to the Rialto to see a cowboy movie and a serial, watch the Saturday shoppers, then walk home. We were normally barefoot, the kids that is, as we rarely wore shoes except in winter. We could not afford them for one thing, and did not want to for another.

Mary was usually catered to and petted by Dan and Ethel, only tolerated by Ivan and Odis. Sometimes tormented, especially when they were left to "baby sit". Occasionally she was forced to chew tobacco as a condition to being helped off the roof. How Mary got up on the roof remains a mystery. Playing in empty box cars on the track was another favorite pastime of the boys, and Mary usually went along.

During this hard time a lot of people were out of work, on relief (something they had during the depression) and lived with relatives. It was not uncommon for families of two generations to live together. Most of the older homes had storm houses, or storm cellars, which were usually spider infested, musty and scary. Unlike the present time, most people dashed to the storm house when "a cloud came up" in those days, and this procedure put fear in my heart for years. One of my worst memories is of Dan's calling for help on a rain swept stormy night, unable to make it to the storm house. Dan suffered severe arthritis and had crippled feet. All her life Mary remembered Daddy wearing high top shoes that had been altered to accommodate the bad toes.

Times never improved much in Mary's childhood, but there was always good food on the table, decent clothes (although never more than one pair of shoes at a time). In fact, although we had electricity we cooked on a wood stove and had an outhouse until Mary's teenage years.

Mary was born on December 13, 1926, in "Bailey's Place" in Red River County near Clarksville. She was brought into the world by a midwife and overseen by Granny Ashley, as all four of Ethel's children were. One son died very young.

The Ashley's had migrated from Gadsden, Alabama, to Clarksville. Like Dan and Ethel, the Ashley's share cropped on the "halves" or "fourths". The landowner allowed them to live in a house on his property, grow crops, and share the profits with the owner. This was a way of life in early Texas.

LIGHTS OUT—By Toni Smith

On November 9th, 1965 our family of seven was living in Reading, Massachusetts. Our house had been built in 1900, sturdy and solid. There was a back and front stairway, a long hallway and roughhewn oak floors upstairs, and doors leading from the hallway to the bedrooms and bathroom. At the end of the hallway was a door leading to a full attic. The downstairs had a parlor, living room, dining room, a large kitchen, and a big pantry. Off the kitchen was what I called the "mud room" with an old fashioned chain-flush toilet.

It was about ten after five, the spaghetti sauce was simmering, the pasta was cooking in the big kettle of boiling water, and except for heating left-over rolls, and shredding some of the cheese, supper was ready. I went to the bottom of the back stairway to call the boys to get cleaned up for supper. "Is Dad home yet?" the youngest one hollered.

"No, but he will be here any minute, and supper is ready." I turned to put the rolls in the oven and check the clock, when the lights went out. *"What did those boys do now?"* I thought. They were always experimenting hooking up some gimmick or other. I put the pan down on what I hoped would be the table and looked in the direction of the window. Pitch Black inside and out. I couldn't see a thing! Scary! This big house, no lights, no heat. Worse than that, no T.V. or Radio! What were the kids going to do, and what was I going to do with the kids? *"Well,"* I thought, *"This won't last long. There's always the phone."* I worked my way to where the phone should be, found it without banging my shin on any chairs or the table. I lifted the receiver. Dead! Not a sound. Now I really was concerned. "Ma! Ma! What happened?" Came a lusty yell from upstairs, "Do I have to finish washing my hands? I can't find the soap!"

"Never mind. Just get down here to help me find some candles." Where are the girls, I thought. I had been so busy that I couldn't remember if they were upstairs or in the parlor watching Dick Clark on T.V. I heard footsteps behind me and let out a yelp, as a hand touched my back. "Mom is that you?" One of the girls whispered. I was so jumpy it took a few minutes to figure out which of the three girls was behind me.

"Where were you?" I asked. "We were upstairs fixing Jannie's hair because Billy is coming over tonight. What do we do now?" "Look for candles," I said. I was trying to sound calm and collected but had no idea at this moment where candles could possibly be.

"But mom, Jannie is having a hissie, cause her hair is a mess. I couldn't see what I was doing when the lights went out and I poured stuff all over her. It was some lotion to make her hair curly and…" "We have more important things to worry about. Her hair will dry. Now get the other two down here, and let's find some candles, now!"

Thump, thump, thump! "Ouch my head! Oh, it must be bleeding! I can't see. Where am I? Where is everybody?" "You hit me!" Sounded a voice from somewhere. "I did not, I bumped you, who are you?"

"Mom, where are you?" "Just calm down!" I tried to sound like someone in complete control although my voice crackled. "Does anyone know where the flashlight is?" "In the car. Dad was looking for his lottery ticket."

"Okay, that takes care of that. Nancy, you take the pantry, Jannie you look in the hutch in the dining room. Where is Cheryl?" "Under her bed. Mom, you know that's where she always goes when there's any trouble or anything scary." "One of you go up and get Cheryl, be nice please. No yelling about being a 'scare-dey' cat. Does anyone know where the dog is?" "Oh, mom, I don't know about Amy, but Jannie's kitten got out this afternoon, and we couldn't find her. What will we do?"

At this point I could not tell where anyone was, or whether all the kids were in the kitchen or some still upstairs. I was going by voice recognition. "Ma, are we all in the kitchen? What was that lumpy thing on the stairs? I can't see anything. I'm not movin' until I know where I am and where everyone else is." Rick hollered from somewhere in the darkness.

"Oh I wish I could see my hair, it feels all gooey. I can't let Billy see me!" Jannie wailed. "He couldn't see you now anyway, gooey-head." "And I'm not going into the dining room, it's too spooky in there."

"Will you all cool it?" I took a deep breath, and as calmly as I could remarked, "I just remembered Grandpa's old railroad lantern is down in the cellar." "I'm not going down there!" Shouted all those gathered in the kitchen, or wherever. "Stop it, I'll go."

I started shaking, thinking about going down those rickety old stairs and bumping into spider webs hanging from those old rafters. "No! Mom, you can't leave us up here in the dark. You might fall, and never come back up." "How will we get any supper if you get lost down there!" whimpered Lee the chronic worrier with the fussy appetite.

I just remembered the spaghetti must be like cement by this time. Maybe that was what I could smell. Everything was still cooking even though the electricity had gone out. Having a gas stove was to prove very fortunate, but at that moment I couldn't think about that. I could hear the kids scrunching around, muttering and grumbling, as I tried to find my way to the cellar door. I had just reached the cellar doorway when car headlights shone through the window from the driveway. Light! Then blackout again as the car lights went out, and the car door slammed shut. The kitchen door flew open. "Anybody home?" My husband hollered, the only answer that could be heard was a loud, long and mournful moan. "Did you bring the flashlight?" A voice came from the darkness.

That was our introduction to the extended visit of the East Coast Blackout!

Footnote: November 9, 1965 was forty one years ago. Within twelve minutes that black out covered seven states and two Canadian provinces; creating eighty thousand miles of total darkness. Those who lived through it have had their stories told in many ways. This was the time of the cold war, and the most frightening aspect of this situation was that the Russians had instigated this – (not true of course) – and everyone was waiting for an air-attack. The following days were ones we all remembered for their compassion, humor, sharing and caring. Those of us with gas stoves were very busy cooking everything and anything we could squeeze on top of the stove or in the oven. Those with BBQ's created delicious smells that permeated the neighborhood. As Judie Glave of "The Orange County Register" paper put it; and I quote: "To many New Yorkers it was a time of jovial inconvenience, one where urban strangers became friends and the city pulled together in an unparalleled cohesiveness." I'm not sure that I, living in Massachusetts, would agree with the "jovial inconvenience." However, congeniality and understanding of one's neighbors helped us all to "Ride the black out!"

LOVER RECONSIDERED
By Gene Guerreno

If, first, I let the sigh escape –

Then the tears would quickly follow;

While lips assumed the mournful shape

Of the Sob … an echoed hollow.

In circumstance so gravely sad,

My tears seem strangely mellow –

And I wonder if it's all that <u>bad</u>,

To lose this tiresome fellow?

How dared he say, " … This Love's passé … " ?

… that inconsequential cad!

Why should I cry? I'll bless the day…

I shed this loathsome lad!

MORNING
By Ellen Canterbury

I have come to the conclusion

That early morning

Is my most

Creative time.

I speak openly to God,

Veiling no innuendoes.

And listen to His words

Of guidance,

Chastisement,

And encouragement.

Then, I move along

Into a daily routine

In a quiet, steady cadence

To face the clatter

And commotion

Of the day.

MUSIC
By Stella Klepac

I care not for the vintages,
Which to the grape belong;
Give me, rather, wine of music
In a vessel of song!
I'll grow drunk on melody.
And debauched with harmony—
The tender passions of Verdi;
Beethoven's mighty voice;
Mozart's gay polyphony;
Strauss' lilting joys;
And Bach sings heavenly beauty;
And Wagner's splendid noise.
…Vintners of consummate skill
Who brew a drink divine –
A melodious intoxication,
A celestial wine!

OLD FOLKS
By George Gardiner

Those of us fortunate enough to be called the "Old Folks," are fortunate indeed. We have experienced things and lived a lifestyle never to be known again. I consider anyone born in the mid thirties, or before, eligible for the label, "Old Folks".

It seems to me those of us raised on a ranch, farm or in a small town are doubly fortunate. How many remember the news that swept the nation… "Lindenberg lands in Paris"? I was a kid on my Granddad's farm in Ohio, dressed as kids of the day: bare footed, Oshkosh B'Gosh overalls, shirt made from a flour sack, and a frizzled straw hat. I listened to my four Uncles discuss the great danger, and the extreme courage of "Lucky Lindy's" solo flight.

Did you ever play Stick Ball with a sawed off hoe handle and a tin can? I had a ball meant to resemble a baseball. It was made of braided rawhide and left in the hot sun to harden. When one of the kids whopped it with a hoe-handle-bat it flew high and far whistling through the air like a locomotive. The ball lasted one summer until Thurman Potee's coon dog, Pretty Boy, found it. That hound chewed on that ball all night. The next morning it looked like a plate of Irish Stew.

Did you ever roll a hoop down the road keeping it going by strokes from a short stick? How about a hot, steamy, summer afternoon when you and all the neighborhood boys headed on the run for the ol' swimming hole, with clothes flung off, with a yip of delight, you did a "cannonball dive" from the bank. Remember how wonderful the cool water felt as you disappeared below the surface?

Remember the day your pet turtle died? Then, while you rocked with your sadness in the front porch swing, Grandma brought you a thick slice of home made bread covered with a thick layer of butter, topped with fresh strawberry jam. Remember threading the strings of popcorn and cranberries for your schoolroom Christmas tree?

Remember the 'in town' Saturday night western movies? Tom Mix, Ken Maynard, Jack Holt, Buck Jones, all with six shooters, big hats, silver studded saddles, and rearing horses. These were the early times of today's "Old Folks".

Young people of today have never breathed the delightful fragrance of new mown alfalfa, or seen a newborn, flat-nosed piglet. Few, if any, of this generation will ever taste made-from-scratch buttermilk flap jacks with lots of melted butter fresh from the churn and covered with brown sugar syrup! Oh, Stop it! I'm drooling.

Yes, we are the "old folks"; we've lived through the good and the bad. What we have experienced, most likely will not come around again. We are known as the "Greatest Generation". We are happy with that. We have had the feast of life, including dessert!

George Erickson—Portrait

PEANUT BUTTER—By Frances McCreadie

As a little girl growing up on a fruit farm, my parents spent little money on such luxuries as oranges and bananas. These were Christmas treats. Indeed, we did not need them with the abundance of apples, berries, peaches and cherries at hand. Those far- away fruits were treated as the luxuries they were. But one treat above all fascinated me, namely peanut butter from some enchanted land. How could such a good tasting, completely different, smooth delicacy come from the same ground as our own garden? My mind lingered on it as did the taste of remembrance. I asked mother if we could buy some peanut butter. "Soon," she said absent mindedly. That was permission to me and I hiked myself to Hoshel's grocery store. I could not see over the counter but Mr. Hoshel was tall. He leaned over the counter until our eyes met.

"I want peanut butter," I told him. "How much?" he said. I had no idea so I said, "Some." He considered that and suggested, "Ten cents worth." "Yes," I said, as if I had meant that in the first place. He placed one of those small wooden tubs on the scale, and placed an oiled paper in it. I watched fascinated as that delicious wonder filled the tub.

"That will be ten cents," he said briskly as he wrapped it carefully and handed it down to me. Ten cents! That was an unforeseen obstacle. I had no money and never had, so what could I say? Mother always came to my rescue so I blurted out, "Mother will pay you some other time."

His smooth face suddenly tightened into a harder line as he said, "Who's mother?" This dissolved me into near panic. "What does your father call her?" he said, and I knew that. "He calls her wifey," I answered, and I knew that. "What does the mailman call her?"

I whispered her name and escaped through the door. Mother was not a regular customer of this particular grocery store, but mothers of necessity have to learn to cope with life. I'm sure she stopped one day at Hoshel's store and as she paid for groceries said casually, "Oh, my little girl came in and bought peanut butter one day so I must pay for that as well."

The stress for me soon faded but the delicious flavor of peanut butter lingered on.

REFLECTIONS
By Ellen Canterbury

Today I returned to old haunts,

To drive again through landscapes so familiar

I remembered an ocotillo in springtime

Flashing suddenly at a bend in the road.

I remembered Datura blossoms

And desert marigold generously

Flaunting their splendor,

The cardinal sang to me

From that very perch four years ago.

But it was harder to find my friends.

Some were deceased,

Others in rest homes,

Or living with children as their caregivers.

Thomas Wolfe was right.

"You can't go home again."

Home is where you presently lodge,

And where you've been has become a memory

To visit in dreams.

SHEPHERD HOUSE—ADAM
By Margaret Benson

Our fifteen year old Apache foster son stood in the middle of our living room. He was livid with anger. My husband, Harry, had just found Adam walking on the roof. In a stern voice he said, "Adam, the roof was not made to walk on, and I don't want you to do that again!"

Adam shouted at Harry, "I've got a knife and I'm going to use it on you!"

What should we do? Neither Harry nor I could physically restrain this angry boy. Something told me to turn on the Hi-Fi. With the flip of a switch, the gospel of John filled the room. I had been listening to it earlier in the day.

Adam stood still for two or three minutes listening. Then he slowly backed up and sat down on the sofa. In a quiet voice he said, "I'm sorry Harry"

Adam did pretty well as a bag boy in the local supermarket. One day he came home after work accompanied by a young couple from Holland. They had asked him if he knew a place they could sleep for a couple of nights, "I told them they could probably stay with us." Fortunately there was a vacant room in Shepherd House, so the Dutch travelers stayed with us for a short time.

Adam was one of many who came to live at Shepherd House in need of help. Establishing this shelter was Harry's new endeavor after 30 years in the ministry. He decided to serve the Lord now by caring for the crippled, mentally challenged, the blind and refugees. He believed that all people had value in God's sight.

To make room for those who needed a home Harry added more rooms to our house, with the help of a retired contractor friend. The demand was so great to live in Shepherd House that Harry soon bought the house next door and enlarged that house as well.

In the 10 years we operated Shepherd House we cared for over 100 people. It was into this Haven that Adam came. In his short life he had been rejected by his mother, and had lived in a dozen foster homes.

He eventually went to high school and returned to the apache reservation. He came back with a friend to visit us. We were out of town, but our son welcomed him warmly. Yes, Adam was valued in God's sight.

SWEET YESTERDAY
By Frances McCreadie

Thread thou lightly on my heart, love,

Bruise it gently, pray;

Promises that shine by moonlight

Lose their glow by day.

Tangled in the threads of music

Songs we used to say

Weaving dreams with magic moonbeams

In a roundelay.

Foolish heart! Leave it behind me

In that far-away.

Let me flee the ties that bind me

Luring me to stay.

I would rather not remember

Let it waft away

Lest there be a lingering fragrance

Of sweet yesterday

THE HIGH COST OF LIVING
By Jeanne Nylander

"The best things in life are free,"

The list may be extensive,

And yet the next best things in life

Are always so expensive

THE NEW NEIGHBOR
By Mary Reeves

The first person I met today was my new neighbor, Libby. What a breath of fresh air she was!!

I had awaked feeling tired and a bit cranky. I pushed the down button (I looked a sight) and wouldn't you know – along comes a stranger.

But not for long! "Good morning" she beamed – "I'm Libby and I just moved in". It was only 6am but Libby seemed to have herself together better than I did – perfect (nothing out of place) as another neighbor had seen it.

Libby, who admitted to being 86, was all smiles and a perfect delight. Can I be her?

THE HOTTEST SPOT
By Fay Bizzell

We left Indio, California at 2:30 in the afternoon not realizing just how terribly hot and dry the desert stretch that lay ahead of us really was. The cool breeze that we had so recently known blowing gently off the Pacific Ocean was soon a thing of the past. Our full realization of the terrific heat came when we were about twenty – five miles out into the arid desert. My husband looked at the temperature gauges on the car panel. The gauge showed a glaring red signal. Now even the car was screaming for relief from the intense heat! The only thing to do was cut our speed to about thirty miles per hour and turn off all the extra power of our '65. Impala and hope we did not get stranded as so many tourists were along the highway. The heat hitting the windshield warmed the glass until one could hardly stand to touch it with bare hands! To roll down the windows was a big mistake. The hot air was like a knife slicing at our throats.

The perspiration trickled down our foreheads like beads of water on a duck. It was too late to turn back now. We must keep going at this snail's pace and hope that the small mid-way station was not too many miles ahead. Being stranded in this desert would be equally as horrifying as being caught in one of the worst blizzards the North had ever known. Finally, the little service station we had hoped for so long appeared on the horizon, but we almost afraid it was a mirage. At the station we parked and let our car engine cool while we had a coke to cool our own engines. The wind was hot standing in the shade of the awning at the station. But we soon found it cooler there than standing in the shade of the building where the wind would blow directly on us. We were soon refreshed and ready to being our travel toward New Mexico. The desert stretched on not too many miles and the temperature change was most welcome. After we arrived home and received the first weather report, we were not too shocked to now that it had been 123 degrees in that area… the hottest spot in the nation!

THE OLD HOME PLACE
By George Gardiner

There are few phrases that stir memories like the words, "The Old Home Place!" It is the house in which you spent your childhood. In your memory the rope swing still hangs from a limb of the shade tree in the side yard. You can see your blue and tallow bike lying by the porch steps where you left it after school.

Bo, the family dog, lies on the porch keeping an eye on a red squirrel frolicking in the yard. The old push lawn mover sets at the end of the house. The house is a tall, square, two-story house with small attic windows up near the roof. There are porches on three sides. Your memory's eye falls on the front porch swing. When you were quite young you tried to see how high you could swing, later years, in the early evening, you curled up on the swing with a pillow, glass of lemonade and a book. A little surge of sweetness moves in the area of your heart as you recall the lovely moments spent on the swing with your "very special person".

You can hear the sounds of living made by your family. Your mother cooking dinner, while she talks with your sister about her day at school. You hear an argument between your brother and your father over who is the better pitcher in the national league… Bo begins to bark as he decides mister squirrel has been in his yard long enough. Can the smell of fried chicken ride the waves of memory? You agree it can as the fragrance of your mother's cooking drifts past your nose. Suddenly you hear the piano music coming from the sitting room. The notes of music have a slight echo coming over time and distance. The song is "Jeannie with the Light Brown Hair."

The stairway you climbed so many times looms in your memory. You can hear the sounds of the night fading one by one. Your mother flicking off the downstairs lights, father calling out, "you kids settle down or I'll be in there!"

Finally, silence… a pleasant country style, quietness settles over the neighborhood. Then …is it in your head, or is it real, the mournful sound of a train whistle, off in the distance? The Silver Streak passenger train goes screaming over Fletcher's crossing every midnight for as long as you can remember. While memory is so willingly ushering you back through the years... the day grandpa and grandma came to live with us. "They just can't make it on their own any more," mother explains. Then one day you came home from school and there is a black wreath on the front door. "Grandma died a little before noon today," your sister whispers.

Next came the funeral held in the front room, with grandma's coffin nearly hidden among the surrounding flowers, mostly gladiolas. The soulful tone of Reverend Oatman's "funeral voice" still lingers from that long ago day.

Then came the happy time of your sister's wedding. Reverend Oatman again, this time with his "wedding voice". Cake, ice cream, laughter, tears, rice, and goodbye hugs. Thing were not quite the same after that day, you remember. The old house had lost one of its own. Things seemed to move very fast after that. You were the first to leave for a job in the big city. It wasn't long until mother and dad were alone. It was early evening when the call came... "Your father passed away this evening," a voice said. "It was sudden, his heart we believe."

As you hung up the phone the reality of the passing years hit home, time was rushing by. After a plan for the care of mother was worked out, the next thing was to put the house up for sale. You remember the emotional blow that hit you when you received word the house had been sold. The home we all loved so much now belonged to someone else! I don't know who bought it, but I do know this... as time rolls on, it will always be "The Old Home Place" to my family and me.

TRIBUTE TO OUR MAILMAN
By George Gardiner

I remember Old Ed, our mailman. Ed Harvey was his name. For years, he delivered the mail driving a horse and buggy. Ed would vary his routine and time a little so as to arrive at a different farmhouse each day. "There's some fried chicken left over from dinner, Ed," grandma would say when Ed handed her the mail. "I allow you're a mite hungry." "A mite, Hatty, and I'm obliged."

While waiting, Ed would lead his horse to a grassy spot in the shade of a tree the set about wiping the dust from his shiny black buggy. Ed would tell Grandma all the news he had picked up along the way as he munched down the fried chicken and cornbread. "Bring me 10 stamps and a pound of coffee when you come by tomorrow please."

"Sure thing, Hatty. Well…. I must be off. Much obliged for the grub, see you tomorrow." That's the way it was all over rural America. RFD. Rural Free Delivery was a blessing to many a farmer or rancher.

One day both grandma and grandpa went out to meet Ed. He was to bring grandma a bottle of vanilla and a box of oatmeal. Grandpa was waiting for a poke of ten-penny nails. I was a six-year-old tag along.

"What in Heavens name is that?" Grandma said as she watched a big cloud of dust rolling towards us. "By jiggers, I believe Ed's mare has kicked the traces and taken off." Grandpa said.

What it was: Ed had bought a 'tin lizzie' (a model T-ford) and wasn't an experienced drier yet. The car with wide-eyed Ed at the wheel came charging at us. Ed swerved off the road and hit one of grandpa's apple trees… Ka-bang! Other than loosing his specs and a knot on his forehead, Ed was all right.

"Just can't seem to remember how to stop this fool contraption." He said as he felt around for his specs. The scar on the tree was still there the last time I went home.

Mary Gleason, known to all as "granny" was Grandma's mother. She was a Civil war widow and as such received a check from the government each month for the sum of twelve dollars. I was with Grandma when she went to meet Ed and get the mail… and the check. As Ed handed Grandma Granny's check he asked, "How is Mary today?" "Mother passed away this morning." Grandma said. Ed didn't hesitate; he reached and took back Granny's check. A look of bewilderment passed across grandma's face.

"I'm sorry Hattie, but it's the law." Ed explained, tucking Granny's check back into his pouch. Twelve dollars to a family back in those days was a heap of money. The lack of it would bring hardship and Ed knew it. Ed got out of the Ford, took Grandma by the arm, and walked over to the well house. They chatted a bit then Ed returned. Just before he drove off he said to me, "Young man, don't you ever tell anyone what you saw here." I never have.

The RFD mailman played a major role in the lives of rural families across America. Aboard a saddle horse or in his buggy, he honored, to the fullest extent, the code of the U.S. postal service, the mail must go through!

Old record show the mailman did far more than deliver the mail. He was known to do everything from bringing a grocery item to getting a check cashed, or treating a snake bite, aiding in rounding up a runaway pig or helping fight a fire; all over and above the call of duty.

He was among the best-loved men in America. A hero, a friend, a role model. I'm told just such mailmen once served Sonoita.

Today by clicking a few buttons on your computer you can send a letter anywhere in the world…. Instantly!! Hey buddy, can you spare a stamp?

TREE CORNER
By Gene Guerreno

The invitation came with a gracious offer of transportation …
Gratefully accepted by answering with my direction…
"Northwest corner … Pima street at Columbus."
"Oh! I know! That's the house set under those Great BIG Trees!"
The great, big trees, indeed …
The great trees that hold as many memories as the
Little, white house.
Trees planted fifty years ago so that the one in front
Could protect the little house… could accommodate
The exuberant, over-wide swing at the corner:
The corner of the country lane that frequently put over-confident
High school aged, new drivers almost inside the
Little white house.
Planted the very small sapling that grew into a GIANT TREE
That protected the little white house on the six-lane road!
Other saplings planted at the same half-century… sweet foliage
The druidic spirits continue to protect, shade and comfort…
The little white house.

WINTER JEWELS
By Stella Klepac

I'll bundle up and out I'll go
Into this wintry night;
For, see there, scattered on the snow
Are diamonds, glittering white.
I see them lying all about
And I shall have to venture out,
The moon is so bright,
There's plenty of light.
Oh, what a happy thing to do,
To gather up a sack or two!

Charles Stone—Blue Daisies

CHAPTER NINE

Down To Earth

While our spirits soar above the clouds, we must eventually come back to earth.

This chapter is dedicated to thoughts and ideas that, while not necessarily lofty are basic and down to earth in content.

CLANCY—By George Gardiner

There was nothing much fancy
About Clancy
He was just a soft-eyed, ginger-colored dog
Who, always in a play for your heart, would win
T'was nothing he said,
Just a turn of the head
And that silly little tongue-lolling grin.

Each morning
His tail wagged the sun up
It was fun up
And running his own private trails
Scaring quails
And lizards with
Long tails.

He made love to bees, nose to nose
On his knees
He'd sniff and smell and blow
When the bloom was low
Then turn and chase a bird in the sky
A mile high
For the moment or so.

He stood alone a lot
In a shady spot
Listening
To the wind in the mesquite
Or the muffled sound of coyote feet
Who were friends of his
Like as not

Often, while others slept in the soothing warm sun
He was on the run
Gathering wonderful smells that lay there
Left by the smells that lay there
Left by the small ones that play there

On the desert floor
As they have there fun.

Clancy's love was big-eyed and strong
And it was wrong
He knew
To go so far away
Beyond the mountain ridge where rabbits play
To a little valley where only animals romp together
Forever And a day.

So with a heart as brave as an astronaut
He fought
To stay a while so his friends
Could go with him
Where the pathway bends
At a Palo Verde tree
Into eternity.

But then, yesterday afternoon
He heard a tune
Whistled by a Saint
Quaint,
But irresistible
So he sent
Running with that dog-like gallop
Tongue near draggin'
Tail a-waggin'.

A bounce, a bound, ears a-floppin'
There is no stoppin' Now;
For he can see
A new land where he
Can run and smell and investigate
And wait,

For you and me.
So long, Clancy,

CONSIDERING
By Charlie Stone

"My you're looking well today!"
Is something people often say,
When what it is they're really meaning
Is really…*"well...considering."*
Unsaid, but always understood
"Considering", had it been used,
Would suggest that they had lied.
Better it's unsaid and just implied.
Where were they many years ago?
Is what I'd really like to know.
That was when they could honestly say
"You are certainly looking well today"
Those years have come and gone so quickly
I've gone from well to sometimes sickly.
But, I've learned to agree with those who say,
How really well you look today!" (Considering)

LADY-IN-WAITING
By Laura Lee McCoy

Sometimes I'm early, I'm seldom late,
Seems like all I do is fidget and wait.
I wait in the morning for the alarm to ring;
I wait by the window for the birds to sing.
I wait for the hair dresser, she's running late.
Seems like waiting is really my fate.
I wait for the postman to deliver the mail.
I get nothing but junk and stuff for sale,
I wait for the elevator to go up or come down.
I wait for the bus to take me to town.
I wait in line at the check out stand,
Clutching my money firmly in hand.
Suddenly out of the restless crowd
Someone hollers very loud;
"Stop that ugly clown,
He almost knocked me down."
As I turn I can see
He's heading straight for me.
I thrust out my trusty walking stick;
He hits the tiles like a ton of brick.
While he lays there on the floor
Cops come in the sliding door.
For me the day turns out fine,
Because now I'm the first in line!

EXCERPTS FROM MEMORIES & IMAGINATION...
My Favorite Hat or Shades of Rudolph Valentino & Velma Banky
By Lorraine Smith

I was walking home form school, or "dawdling" as my mother would say. Thinking about the new hat Moms said I could have this year. My old skimmer was about three years old, quite worn and it was just a week and a half until Easter. It was April in Chicago with a false sense of Spring. Unexpectedly, I saw my Dad sitting on the front porch, his shoulders slumped dejectedly. Dad had a huge shock of black hair, green eyes and though he was slight of build, he sizzled with energy. With a sense of emergency, I hastened my steps and scurried up the concrete steps to the tiny porch. It could just accommodate the hanging swing Dad was sitting on.

It was then I noticed the bright scarlet sign on the front porch proclaiming "Quarantine" and saw the signature of our Health Commissioner, Herman N. Bundesen. Dad motioned me to sit next to him, then explained that Moms was very ill and only the Doctor would be allowed to see her. She had Scarlet Fever and I would have to stay at my Grandmothers' house until Mom was well enough to have the quarantine lifted.

We paused in our conversation while a train thundered by. An automatic reaction as we had lived next to the railroad tracks as long as I could remember. I never really noticed the noise or reverberation of the engines since I was so accustomed to them. The area in which we lived contained small bungalows separated by gangways, with a small patch of yard in the back and even smaller patches in front. Most of our neighbors were of Danish decent. Our name was Olsen. My best friend was Arline Nystrom, another friend Edith Martenson, and the fourth friend Margaret Tomchaney who lived in the Polish section at North Crawford streets. Crawford received the new name of "Pulaski" in honor of the Polish general. As well as being politically expedient for the local committeeman, this would insure his popularity with the Polish folks in the district.

Our ward heeler was Mr. Mitchell, he lived just around the corner from us. We called on him with questions about gasoline stamps; barking dogs; raucous parties; or political inquires. He in turn would suggest exactly how our voting should be directed. It was he who suggested that I not enter the house, thereby escaping the quarantine. It was truly the time of the Last Great Hurrah.

Dad handed me my street car fare of seven cents and two mils. The mils were sold by the street car company who wanted to raise the fare but dared not raise it a whole cent, so they sold ten mils for a penny and raised the fare two mils. I was very concerned about my mother but relished staying with my Grandma and Granddad. Grandma was a very short woman— just five feet tall, and as wide as she was tall.
She wore her coarse black hair in a braid down her back, a heritage of her part Indian ancestry; also the reason my Dad only had to shave once a week. In sharp contrast, Granddad was a burly six foot two. He looked fierce but was the most gentle man I ever knew. I looked forward to spending time with them, mostly because they seemed to like having me around.

Since the day was so pleasant, I opted to walk the five miles or so to Madison and Kedzie, where my grandparents lived. I crossed under the viaduct that separated the next section, which was Italian. It smelled wonderfully of the huge sandwiches on Italian bread, piled high with meats and cheeses and slathered with olive oil sold at the little delis in that section. Also along the way to Grandma's house, I passed the Garfield Park Conservatory. I always made a side trip to this wonderful place and wandered through it with the awe only a city girl could have for things that grow.

At last I arrived at Grandma's. They were very poor but I never realized this. I slowly walked up to their third floor cold-water flat. Grandma was already in the hall. "Where in the world have you been girl? I've been waiting for you for an hour." "I walked Grandma" I replied. She gave me a big hug and beckoned my inside. She gave me root beer and cookies.

The front room in which I slept was not often used. They kept it closed to conserve the heat. The cold was penetrating except in the summer, but I never really minded as Grandma would heat up one of her irons on the pot-bellied stove in the kitchen. The irons had a handle you switched to the next iron when the first iron got cold. She would wrap one of these irons in a towel and put it at the foot of the bed and I would feel all cozy and cared-for.

While I was very concerned about my mother, I had another problem. It was about my hat, my new Easter hat. I knew I had to talk to my folks about it. I still had the seven cents Dad had given me. A telephone call was five cents so I went down to the corner drugstore where they had a telephone to call home. Grandma didn't have a telephone but my folks did. It was sometimes difficult to get through as we had a four party line. I felt very lucky when Dad answered right away. When Dad told me that Moms was doing very well, I was somewhat relieved. I explained my hat problem to Dad and he conferred with Moms. She suggested that I use her credit at Carson Pierie Scott & Co. which was a downtown store and I could spend as much as five dollars on the hat of my choice. Grandma agreed to take me downtown the very next day.

Grandma and I started off on one of the two streetcars that would take us downtown. We arrived about an hour later and went immediately to the department store, then upstairs to the millinery department. What a feast for the eyes. There were boxes of hat frames, roll upon roll of colored ribbons, crates of feathers and beads. I knew that I could have my choice. Then from across the room I spied it—The Hat– in all of it's oriental splendor. I knew if Velma Banky were to put on that hat, Rudolph Valentino would sweep her off her feet in a mad passionate embrace, rolling his big black expressive eyes with desire. I was somewhat surprised that Grandma did not immediately see how perfect that hat was for me. I believe she was thinking in terms of another skimmer, with perhaps a flower or a different colored ribbon. This hat was a turban, with a large circle of beads draped over each side, a lovely feather, and a nose length provocative veil. It took a bit of enthusiastic persuasion for Grandma to surrender, but at last the hat was mine. I wore my new hat to church and my buddy, Arline agreed that this was truly a divine hat.

In another day or two Moms was well enough for the Quarantine sign to come down. It was nice to be home again. Mother said very little about my new hat. I did notice when we went to church, or rode the el or street car, she somehow managed to sit a little distance away. She also encouraged me to wear it in the rain. Of all the hats I've owned since that long time ago, none has inspired me with such passion.

MERRY BIRTHDAY
by Gene Guerreno

A Christmas Birthday's the very worst!

Happy the Tenth or the Thirty-First …

In between … from the Twenty-Second -

'One for both' most Donors reckoned:

Stick Birthday Card on Christmas gift -

The birthday kid keeps getting stiffed!

Day-after Collapse! Forget Twenty-Six -

Twenty-Four gets lost in the 'last minute' fix.

Baby Jesus takes over Twenty-Five …

Birthday gets lost—keeping Christmas alive.

On the other hand … One must admit

You get the World celebrating it!

Sagittarian … for three weeks before -

Capricorn … for one week more.

When Birthdays come wrapped in Christmas Cheer -

I guess it's the happiest day of the year!

MERRY OCTOBER FIRST
by Gene Guerreno

The months, in their years, mark Halloween

At the end of October - but I've just seen

A shining Christmas Tree - windowed there

On October one! Shop <u>Now!</u> No time to spare.

Who stole Thanksgiving? ... Novembers day!

I'm counting one short - the one where we pray!

Innkeepers renting the stable now?

Crèche thrown in with Magi and Bow?

Autumn Angels to sing peace and good will—

To men on earth ... fighting still!

Merry October! ... Whoopee Holidays!

To celebrate the Star's bright rays!

NEWCOMER
By Ellen Canterbury

Do you adopt the land,

Or does the land reach out?

Do you say, "This land is mine?"

Or is it the other way around?

The land possessing you?

I like to think it is the land

That has adopted me.

Charles Stone—Desert Quail

OTHER COUSINS AND OTHER BROTHERS
By Mary Reeves

William Kelly Holt (Memories of wife Louise and daughter Edna)—In Louise's recounting their life together on the anniversary of their 50th year together, she begins "Bill was the handsomest man in the country and I was the happiest girl", he was 6'2" in height, 184 lbs. and "had the cutest ways".

They were married April 8, 1925 at the courthouse in Clarksville with momma (Sadie) attending. They had lunch in town, then spent their first night of marriage at her parents' house. The next day they moved into their own little cottage, described as "an old fashioned house with roses and honeysuckle vines". And every Saturday night they would go visit her parents on "Bailey's Place".

All the Holt boys were big and strong, honest and dependable, and caring. Louise recounts Bill's concern when his sister Mary died, leaving a newborn and a six year old boy. He was not allowed to keep the little boy, Zeke, himself but made sure he had a good home.

After they married Bill bought Louise a guitar and taught her to chord on it. He himself, like many of the Holts , was musically inclined by nature. This coupled played for many a dance and had money thrown at them to keep them playing.

They got to travel a bit in West Texas as they were lucky enough to have a 1917 Ford! Then, as Louise put it, mother nature took a hand and their first little girl was born. She was followed by nine more siblings!

While pregnant with the first child Louise tells of their driving through Lubbock. She wanted a hat but was ashamed to show herself, being pregnant. Well, Bill just went into the store and bought her one. She vehemently stated it looked like a chamber pot and threw it out the door. Bill screeched the tires, turned around, went back for the hat and got his money back. No Holt ever loses money if they can help it!

RE-CYCLE
By Ellen Canterbury

It's a little plastic bag
which could be used
for something:
For odd buttons, random jewelry,
or cancelled postage stamps
to send to an orphan's home
Instead, I twist it into nothing,
tie a knot with it,
Now, I can throw it away
As it is good for nothing.

Ann Mari Brandt—Girl in the Garden

THE DRUID FACTOR
By Gene Guerreno

It was not until after I had moved into my apartment that I realized that the lovely tree, just outside, would make the rooms darker. No matter. I have a long-going affair with trees; I'd rather turn on more lights than to forsake my tree. As the desert monsoon season progresses, the tree and its shadows grow more important.

…a tree is a tree…is a tree…is a tree… until, one day, having nothing better to read, the thumb flipped over to the later pages of the Fourth grade Reader, and "TREES" popped up. That's Joyce Kilmer's famous poem, and an idle read-through changed, forever, the way in which one small person would see trees. Any tree. All trees. … and may the Literary critics who cry , "UGH!" be compelled to fry in Hell forever and eternally, fighting forest fires.

There is, currently, a tragic curse of contagious disease destroying thousands of the magnificent Elm trees that, at one time, grew so prolifically in the American countryside. There is a very small hope for treatment that may exist, where there was none before. For now, we will treasure, in our minds and hearts, those special ones we knew best. Hey! That's the one! The BIG one! So strategically placed for one to slip out after bedtime … or maybe the one you fell from and broke your arm… you hurried that one too much! … The one shading the mumbling creek in the pasture, or maybe the one that grew by the school with all the carved initials, optimistically, with the promise to old men who return, that they did, indeed, go with the others who carved.

Wasn't there usually a Grandfather Elm occupying a major portion of childhood's perimeters? Did the 'tree-hugger' manage to slow down some of the bull-dozing as they crashed through the developer's schemes? Are any of the elms still sheltering Fourth of July and Labor Day feasts?

Praise to the 'Ent"! The solemn, magnificent creation of J.R.R. Tolkien … The TREE of all trees; majestically inducting us into our Novitiate of Adoration. The 'Ent' … graciously permitting the impertinence of various rope-hung appurtenances the attached themselves to an inviting lower branch … your trapeze bar and rings … the board seat fitted into the looped rope, where a questing toe could set up the gentle sway that promoted … Thinking … Thought … Big Stuff … the stuff of dreams. Growing a bit older, you and the ENT … the great trunk and a branching into a fork. Beckoning and whispering, 'if someone were to fetch mats and pillows there's a place – right there- to nestle into that triple fork'. Creeping into the great arms for a nap and a dream. Hear that softly swished, murmuring lullaby! … and the breeze chatting with the moving leaves about far-away places and exotic manners. Conversational Enchantment and Temptation, if you speak 'TREE' … and who doesn't?

The thought that naturally follows …

"Isn't there a ladder in the garage?"

"Nah! Too heavy."

"Boxes?"

"Too light."

"Board!"

There's a board plank. Long -sturdy—light enough to drag…the obvious destiny of that plank is to be leaned against that tree—properly angled for creeping up…somewhere back there…

"WELL. YES!"

"Go with GOD!"

"DRUIDS! EN GARDE!"

"BE WELL, GRANDFATHER!"

THE FIRST TIME I SAW QUEEN ELIZABETH
By Mary Reeves

A few years ago our whole family went to London to attend the wedding of my grandson who happens to live in London.

I arrived one day before the family, so I checked into our hotel and since we were staying at Westminster Village, I decided I would go to Westminster Abbey for a tour. When I arrived I never saw so many people standing about, surrounding the place. I asked a Brit, "Why isn't the Abbey open?" "Oooooo! We are waiting for Her Majesty!!!"

Well, I got as close as I could with my camera ready, and was fortunate to get a really good place to see the action. First the Canadian P.M. and his wife arrived in a big black car...got out and shook hands with the Archbishop and went inside. About 20 minutes passed and a really big black care arrived with flags, and out stepped Elizabeth and Philip..she was all doodied out in blue from head to toe. I have heard there is not one thing in that purse she carries....in spite of the screaming , did she turn her head even slightly or wave, to acknowledge such adoration? No!!! She put her hand out to greet the Archbishop and in they went. How rude I say.

I got a really good shot of her backside and side profile, but not her face. The next day in Westminster Village I thought I saw her blue hat in a thrift shop...My family could not get over me seeing the Queen so casually as all of them had lived there at one time and never saw her. I was really looking forward to seeing that famous wave.

THE PROPHETIC INDIAN CHIEF—By Charlie Stone

T'was October and the Indians were worried.
Was the coming winter to be mild and cold?
So they went to the chief
In hopes of relief,
Knowing they'd believe whatever they're told.
Now the chief was just fresh out of college.
And the tribal secrets he'd never been taught.
So he furrowed his brow
And pronounced as to how
Very cold the winter would be, he thought.
He folded his arms, and tried to look wise
And they knew what he'd say would be true.
"Gather up firewood,
As much as you could,
And once that's been done, that's all you can do!"
Then the chief got to worrying and wondering
Is it possible he'd have spoken too fast?
Perhaps, to be certain
He'd just call that person
He knew at the Bureau of Weather Forecast.
The Bureau was happy to share what they knew.
That the winter was going to be cold.
The chief was relieved
That he hadn't deceived
All his brothers by what they have been told.
And he called all the tribe together again
To repeat what he'd told them to do.
With considerable relief
He confirmed his belief
That they would gather even more firewood, too!
Sometime later, the chief got to worrying
Might the Bureau have been a bit hazy?
And the answer they told
Was "We know it'll be cold,
Because the Indians are gathering firewood like crazy!"

THE MAGIC WAND
By Toni Smith

Penny left her friend's house in a worried state of mind. It was very late in the afternoon, and the gathering dusk made her surroundings look rather eerie. It was getting dark, and the slush and snow from yesterday's storm was fast freezing under foot. The neighborhood she lived in was old with large thick hedges surrounding peoples' property and many knarled oak trees whose drooping branches hung low over the sidewalks. The brick bungalows were close together with their window curtains closed against the winter cold. Dark shadows darted around her and the wind whistled through the frozen leaves on the trees.

Penny wasn't very tall, and rather chubby. She was wearing a heavy wool lined coat, mittens, and a scarf tied around the lower part of her face. A hand knitted wool hat, kept sliding down over her forehead. All those burdensome clothes and buckled galoshes made it difficult to walk very fast. It was getting later and darker and she knew she was in trouble with her mother. She was late. Nothing could change that!

Darkness had settled now, and because there were no porch lights, and no street lights, the surrounding houses took on weird shapes. Not many cars drove by because not many people in her neighborhood owned cars. Because of the darkness, Penny was surprised to find herself in front of her house, but was in no hurry to go in knowing how upset her mother would be. There was a scrunching noise behind her. Hesitating to go in, she turned around to see if she could tell what it was. As it came closer she thought it might be the neighbor's dog, who was very friendly. She slowly turned around. Penny could barely see someone walking toward her through the darkness. Whoever it was carried a long pole. She could see there were street lamps shining brightly behind him. She took a deep breath and smiled. Of course, Mr. Lamp Lighter. How exciting to be out in front of her house when he arrived. Slowly, as the lights came on, one at a time, the shadows became trees, shapes became houses and she could clearly see her house.

Mr. Lamp Lighter walked slowly with his long pole tucked closely to his side. He was dressed for the cold weather with a scarf high around his face. As he came close to the lamp pole in front of her house, he glanced over and saw Penny, and gave a small wave with his empty hand. He then turned, placed one foot on a small metal lip at the bottom of the lamp post, reached up and opened a glass door near the top of the post. He tipped the pole just inside the little glass door. A tiny blue flame appeared. It grew bigger then burst into candle shaped glow. It was like watching something magical. Reaching up slowly, he closed the door, stepped down, and waved again moving on through the shadows to the next lamp.

Penny looked up and saw a light in the front window of her house. Her mother and father were looking out at her. She hesitated, but didn't mind going inside now. She had seen light appear as a magic wand wove it's spell making all eerie shadows around her disappear. She looked back and could see all the twinkling street lamps through the darkness. Mr. Lamp Lighter had disappeared in the outer shadows. She know he would come back again. Penny would patiently watch and wait for Mr. Lamp Lighter to turn darkness into light with his magical wand.

THE SKY MAY BE FALLING ...SHOULD WE TELL THE KING?
By Charlie Stone

The debate about global warming has become a sort of litmus test that turns us red or blue depending on our party affiliation. The red states (conservative) feel the extent of global warming is exaggerated and, regardless of whatever the results of this warming might be, it is an acceptable price to pay to save the expenses which would be incurred by the gas, coal and oil industries.

The blue states (Liberal) believe the damaging effects of global warming will be catastrophic not only to the economy, but to the entire planet s well. And the cost to correct the trend is not only acceptable, but absolutely necessary.

What is global warming?

Global warming is the result of an increase in carbon particles in the atmosphere. There has been a critical balance for billions of years, maintaining the 240 to 270 ppm (particles of carbon per million meters of air). These carbon particles collect like a blanket surrounding the earth. If the blanket gets too thick (around 440 ppm), the earth gets too warm, glaciers melt causing devastating floods, while crops burn from the heat resulting in wide spread food shortages. Insects are known to increase their populations as the temperatures rise causing further damage to crops.

Results of Global warming

Even now, the signs are beginning to show. The three hottest years in recorded history have occurred since 1998. Ocean temperatures are rising. Wild fires are more frequent and intense. Last year floods caused hundreds of million of dollars of damage while drought created severe dust storms in the U.S. In 1958 the ppm level was 316. The 2003 level was 375! Most scientists agree that the magic number is 440. That's the point of no return. Then it may be too late for the planet to correct itself to a habitable balance.

What can we do about it?

In 1997 an international accord was reached setting limits for

CO2 atmospheric levels called the Kyoto Agreement. It called for all the developed nations to return their CO2 levels to their levels of 1990. The agreement was signed by George W. Bush's father and ratified by the Senate.

However, in 2001, the administration announced his opposition to Kyoto, saying the damage of global warming was greatly exaggerated and the economy could not afford

to meet the Kyoto standards. To justify this stand the administration cities articles extolling the benefits to plant life with an increase of CO2 in the air. These articles are often financed by coal companies and ignore the preponderance of studies warning us of the disastrous consequences to the earth.

Those who are inclined to agree with the administration's indifference to this issue like to minimize the extent to which our use of fossil fuel has contributed to global warming. The facts, however, are otherwise. There is a direct correlation between the industrial revolution and Co2 increases in the atmosphere. And, as our appetite for energy from fossil fuel increases, so will our atmospheric pollution.

We're not asking the right question

If alien anthropologists were to study life forms on earth they would conclude that there is only one species that soils its own nest ... Homo Sapiens. The Kyoto Agreement offers the best solution for solving this impending crisis. Paraphrasing Chicken Little, "The Sky is falling ... should we tell the King?" The administration has already been told. But they either refuse to believe there's a problem, or simply don't want to address the problem on their watch! In either case, they should be made aware that we do care.

When "can we afford to sign the Kyoto Agreement?" is asked, it's not the right question. The real question is "can we afford not to?" Red or blue, conservative or liberal, we all share the same planet. It's the only one we have!

THE TEMPERANCE SERMON
By Charlie Stone

The preacher was grim
And his message was grimmer …
That beer, wine, and, whiskey
Should be poured in the river.
"If I had my way,
All the beer I could find
Would be poured in the river,
Along with the wine."
"And all of the whiskey,
I'd put in the river …
Every quart, every drop
To the very last jigger!"
It was then he sat down
And saw with chagrin
What the choir had chosen
For the following hymn.
The choir stood up
And performed with a vigor
As their voices sang loudly
"Shall we gather at the river?"

TRAVEL ON THE AIRLINE
By Ellen Canterbury

"I have to take my pill", she said
As she searched for a drinking fountain in the terminal.
Starbucks coffee, coke machine, juice, but where was the water?

A dollar was a tip, now it's a pittance.
Heaven forbid that I should live when ten dollars is a tip!

Angels come in all shapes and sizes.
A young man, Dan, with tousled hair, pushed my wheelchair,
Untied my shoes, replaced them, placed my check-in items in the bin.
Then gave me a friendly grin and a high five
Before he left me on his way to another destination.

To read on the airline is to miss what goes on around you,
People watching, landscapes appearing and disappearing ,
Clouds in myriad billows, puffing and blowing in celestial breezes.
And so it is, I return to my reading.
One pleasure after another!

Now I return to home landscapes.
I have been gone and in those endless days time stood still.
I reveled in endless time, now I return.
The dreaming is over.
Reality returns to what was before.

WARNING
By Marion Brown

Earth is giving constantly,
To sustain you and me.
We've taken and taken
Not looking to see,
How we've plundered her
Relentlessly.
Rachel Carson gave warning,
Was by many perceived
As a doomsday sayer:
From her sense taken leave.
Now many years later
While looking askance,
We must decide
If we've another chance.
To replenish
And bring nature
Again,
Into Balance.

Wilda Hall—Still Life In Blues

Charles Stone—The Eagle

CHAPTER TEN

In The Spirit Of Appreciation

In this book we have compiled thousands of words testifying to the soaring spirit of Fellowship Square residents "...as if raised on the wings of eagles."

But, words are inadequate when it comes to expressing how sincerely appreciative we are of the many employees, opportunities and services fellowship Square provides to make our lives here more comfortable and worthwhile. The following pages are our way of simply saying "Thank You!"

WITH APPRECIATION

The Golden Quill Pen Club is grateful to the many creative contributors to this volume. The represent a rich resource of talent and inspiration which adds beauty, pathos and humor to this chapter of our lives. The opportunity to share with you the reader is part of their reward for their efforts. This could not have been possible without the generous cooperation of the Administration of Fellowship Square Tucson. We are especially grateful to Executive Director, Wendy Capullo, and Marketing Coordinator, Carolyn Roberts-Gorst for all of their support in developing this volume as an avenue to reveal the "good life" we all enjoy at FST.

The Golden Quill Pen Club wishes to acknowledge its special debt to its President Toni Smith for her untiring efforts in pursuing this venture to s successful conclusion. We realize we could not have accomplished this effort without her able leadership. Thank-you.

The Golden Quill Pen Club,
Fellowship Square, Tucson

THE LEGACY OF THE CROOKED TREE OF FELLOWSHIP SQUARE
By George Gardiner
With respect and admiration for Charlie Stone

We met one summer afternoon,
Beneath the crooked tree

On campus of Fellowship Square,
He had stopped to speak to me.

"There is poetry in old trees" he said,
"And music in their leaves.

It's fragrance lies upon the earth,
And sweetens the air mankind breaths

This crooked tree has been a friend,
But not the years have slipped quickly by,

No longer will we share the shade,
Or hear the gentle wind sing and sigh.

This tranquil old tree soon will pass...as soon will I,
I'll reach out and take the hand of God,

And walk into the sky."
He stepped to my side, and held out his hand.

"It may be," he said, "you wish to be alone.
So, until we meet again...my name is Charlie Stone."

Now God has taken the man and taken the tree,
Leaving their poetry and their music,
For you and for me.

TO CHARLES STONE, WITH GRATITUDE

It was just a couple of years ago that Charles and Mary Lou Stone became residents at Fellowship Square, Tucson. Being avid bridge players it was not long before they were sought out be fellow players and soon admired for their skills. Then, at one of the resident sales events, Charles revealed his artistic and printing skills (the latter, his former occupation) with the display of his note and Christmas Cards. These were in high demand and led to the exposure of his talent as an artist. His paintings of birds and flowers (his favorite subjects) rival the best in the field as noted by the eagle depicted on our cover, designed by him.

It is said that most people indulge in discussion about other people or events but great minds discuss ideas. Charles' interest in ideas led him to the area of poetic expression. He immersed himself in studying the techniques of creating poetry and after indulging creatively in the act, helped inspire the Golden Quill Pen club to expand its interests in this direction. In a short time, his influence was felt and appreciated by all.

The ego has a propensity of labeling, the Soul appreciates. Charles was a great appreciator of all of life, especially natures' beauty, his wife, their family and friends. An old expression says, "That a man is wise who sees life through the eyes of a child. Whether at its beginning or , life will be his friend."

Life is your friend, Charles, and we are privileged to call you ours. Thank you for sharing yourself and your gifts.

The Golden Quill Pen Club

THANKS FOR THE OPPORTUNITY
By Francis McCreadie

I am so happy to have an opportunity to thank those people (you know who you are) who have worked so tirelessly behind the scenes to help bring to fruition our dreams of actually publishing a book. It is certainly stimulation and pleasing to see one's name in print. For this too, I think the Activities Department is to be commended for giving us publication each month in the Villager. Where else could we as a group get this exposure?

I've been a member now for more than a year and each meeting has been an encouragement and an inspiration to me. We are welcomed with no judgments on our talents. I'm glad they allowed me to enter the group. Thank you again for all I have received.

THANK YOU TO ALL OUR CONTRIBUTORS:

Phyllis Amos

Joe Apell

Margaret Benson

Fay Bizzell

Ann Mari Brandt

Marion Brown

Alvin Brewer

Ellen Canterbury

Jeanne Chavanelle

Ralph Dorff

George Erickson

Ann Fouratt

Chuck Fouratt

Victoria Franks

George Gardiner

Trudy Gordon

Gene Guerreno

Wilda Hall

Suzanne Harvor

Elsie Hobbs

Stella Klepac

Dottie Kath

Bob Lockwood

Mimi Lloyd

Lois Ladwig

Aileen Mercurio

Frances McCreadie

Laura Lee McCoy

Jean Nylander

Arlene Radek

Mary Reeves

Rosemary Sample

Penny Sarno

Lorraine Smith

Oreita Smith

Toni Smith

Ruth Spitzer

Bernice Steinhauser

Elsa Stiger

Red Stolle

Charles Stone

Evelyn Wilson

Along with all of the residents who so generously shared their stories and experiences with us in interviews, to publish.